TWAYNE'S WORLD AUTHORS SERIES
A Survey of the World's Literature

SPAIN

Janet W. Díaz, Texas Tech University
EDITOR

Fernando Arrabal

TWAS 499

Fernando Arrabal

FERNANDO ARRABAL

By PETER L. PODOL
Lock Haven State College

TWAYNE PUBLISHERS
A DIVISION OF G. K. HALL & CO., BOSTON

Library of Congress Cataloging in Publication Data

Podol, Peter L
Fernando Arrabal.

(Twayne's world authors series ; TWAS 499 : Spain)
Bibliography: p. 167–73
Includes index.
1. Arrabal, Fernando—Criticism and interpretation
PQ6601.R58Z8   842'.9'14   78–18009
ISBN 0–8057–6340–6

Contents

About the Author

Peter L. Podol is Professor of Spanish at Lock Haven State College in Pennsylvania. He received his B.A. from the University of Pennsylvania, his M.A. from Columbia University, and his Ph.D. from the University of Pennsylvania. He formerly taught at Lincoln University and at Dickinson College. Professor Podol's specialty is Spanish drama, and he has contributed articles and reviews to *Hispania, Hispanic Review, Revista de estudios hispánicos, Estreno, Hispanófila, Studies in Twentieth Century Literature, West Coast Review,* and *Explicación de textos literarios.* He has also prepared an essay entitled "The Grotesque Mode in Contemporary Spanish Theater and Film" for publication in a volume of essays devoted to the grotesque.

Preface

When Fernando Arrabal emigrated from Spain in 1955 and entered self-imposed exile in Paris, he was twenty-two years old, physically sick, and largely unknown as a dramatist in his native country. Using the bizarre events of his wartime childhood as a source of inspiration, Arrabal began to produce a form of avant-garde drama that utilized a number of the artistic currents prevalent in Paris; but he managed to retain his Spanish sensibility and his individuality. His plays shocked and provoked his audiences and initially alienated many of the drama critics; but eventually he began to attract a following. The frequently hostile reviews that his plays continued to receive excited the interest of theatergoers and expanded his audience. After the foundation of the Panic Movement in 1962, he began to work with more talented directors and to come into contact with the most stimulating minds in contemporary avant-garde theater. By the late 1960s, his reputation was assured; he had become the most performed playwright in Paris. He has remained a controversial writer and personality, but has also succeeded in winning worldwide recognition.

The present study emphasizes Arrabal's theater, but also considers his work in other genres. It is intended to elucidate the central focus of his drama, to demonstrate how the structure and thematic content of his plays reflect a dialectical tension that exists in his own personality and manifests itself in his theater in the struggle between hope and despair, love and hatred, reality and illusion. Arrabal's plays blend the personal and the political, the psychological and the sociological, into a unified quest for self-understanding and liberation.

No book has yet been published that deals with all of the writer's works, and none of any kind has been done in English. In this work, translations, unless otherwise indicated, are my own. It is my hope that this study, which will introduce to English speaking readers the first Spanish playwright since Lorca to gain international recognition, will also prove to be of interest to specialists in both Spanish and French contemporary theater.

PETER L. PODOL

Lock Haven State College

Acknowledgments

The author particularly wishes to express his appreciation to Fernando Arrabal whose willingness to discuss his work and whose cooperation in examining the accuracy of this study's chronology were invaluable assets in the preparation of the manuscript. The author must also thank Angel Berenguer of The State University of New York at Albany for his assistance in arranging for several of my interviews with Arrabal. And the helpful criticism of my editor, Janet Díaz, was most appreciated. Finally, special thanks are in order to my wife, Jo, whose patience, understanding and editorial assistance made this book possible.

Chronology

1932   August 11: Fernando Arrabal born in Melilla, Spanish Morocco, to Fernando Arrabal Ruiz and Carmen Teran González.

1936   July 17: The Spanish Civil War breaks out in Spanish Morocco; Arrabal's father, arrested by the Nationalists, is sentenced to death. His family moves to Ciudad Rodrigo, to reside with Arrabal's grandparents. All references to his father are suppressed; his image is excised from the family photographs.

1937   His father's sentence is commuted to thirty years' imprisonment. Arrabal attends a school run by the Teresiana nuns.

1940   The family moves to Madrid.

1941   Arrabal begins studies at the San Anton School. On December 4, his father is transferred to the Central Hospital of Burgos.

1942   His father escapes from the hospital in his pajamas, and is never found or heard from again.

1947   Arrabal begins the preparatory course at the Military Academy, also discovers the cinema and the works of Lewis Carroll.

1949   The discovery of his father's letters and photographs provokes a crisis in Arrabal who refuses to speak to his mother for five years. Military studies are abandoned. He is sent to Tolosa as an apprentice at the Theoretical-Practical School of the Paper Industry directed by the Escolapians.

1951   Arrabal passes the Baccalaureate examination at Valencia.

1952   He returns to Madrid, commencing the study of law, while working in the paper industry. Arrabal frequents the Ateneo and reads avidly Kafka and Dostoievsky. He writes *Los soldados (Picnic on the Battlefield)* and joins the avant-garde group called Postismo.

1953   *Los hombres del triciclo (The Tricycle)* wins second prize in a playwriting contest in Barcelona.

1954 Arrabal hitchhikes to Paris to see Brecht's *Mother Courage* performed by the Berlin Ensemble; later meets a young French student of Spanish literature named Luce Moreau.

1955 Arrabal writes *Fando and Lis*. Discovers theater of Ionesco and Beckett. In December, leaves for France on a government grant to study theater for three months. Arrabal arrives in poor health and is admitted to the hospital of the Cité Universitaire.

1956 Ill with tuberculosis in the Sanatorium of Bouffemont, except for the few days in November when he undergoes surgery at the Foch Hospital. *Cérémonie pour un Noir assassiné (Ceremony for an Assassinated Black), Le Labyrinthe (The Labyrinth)* and *Les Deux Bourreaux (The Two Executioners)* are written. While hospitalized, he develops his passion for chess.

1957 Confined to the Sanatorium through May, Arrabal writes feverishly; obtains a contract for publication of all his works with Julliard.

1958 *The Tricycle* is performed in Madrid on January 29 at the Teatro de Bellas Artes by the Theater group Dido Pequeño. Arrabal marries Luce Moreau February 1, subsequently tours as an actor in plays of Kafka and Ionesco. During his travels he is reunited with his mother.

1959 His first novel, *Baal Babylone,* is published January 21. *Picnic on the Battlefield,* his first play staged in France, is presented April 25 under the direction of Jean Marie Serreau. November 4 Arrabal departs for the United States on a Ford Foundation grant.

1962 Arrabal's meetings with Jodorowsky, Topor and Sternberg at the Café de la Paix culminate in February with the foundation of the Panic Movement. Arrabal meets André Breton, publishes in the Surrealist revue *La Brèche*.

1963 Arrabal lectures on the "Panic Man" in Sydney, Australia. The first painting commissioned by him, realized by the artist Arnaiz, is entitled: *Arrabal combattant sa megalomanie (Arrabal Combatting his Megalomania)*.

1964 *Le Grand Cérémonial (The Grand Ceremonial)* is staged by Georges Vitaly. Arrabal receives the Lugne Poe Prize for the year.

1966 *Le Cimetière des Voitures (The Car Cemetery* or *The Automobile Graveyard*) is staged in Dijon by Victor García.

Arrabal in Madrid writes *L'Architecte et l'Empereur d'Assyrie (The Architect and the Emperor of Assyria)*, and *Arrabal celebrando la ceremonia de la confusión (Arrabal Celebrating the Ceremony of Confusion)* is published.

1967   *The Architect and the Emperor of Assyria* is staged at the Théâtre Montparnasse-Gaston-Baty under the direction of Jorge Lavelli. Arrabal is arrested on July 21 and imprisoned in Spain, being acquitted in September.

1968   Christian Bourgois continues publication of Arrabal's theater. The first volume of the review *Le Théâtre,* directed by Arrabal, appears in April. In May, Arrabal participates in the Paris student rebellions.

1969   Victor García's production of *The Two Executioners* in Madrid is destroyed by the police on February 11. On April 15 he departs for the United States where he writes *Et ils passèrent des menottes aux fleurs (And They Put Handcuffs on the Flowers),* staged September 20 at the Théâtre de l'Epée de Bois.

1970   *Viva la muerte (Long Live Death)* filmed in Tunisia. His daughter Lelia is born on January 14.

1971   *The Architect and the Emperor of Assyria* is produced at the National Theater of London under the direction of Victor García.

1972   His son Samuel is born on July 15. Directs *And They Put Handcuffs on the Flowers* in New York.

1973   Release of the film *J'irai comme un cheval fou (I Would Go Like a Crazy Horse),* based on *The Architect.*

1974   Visits Madrid, New Mexico, in April; writes *En la cuerda floja o la balada del tren fantasma (On the Wire or The Ballad of the Phantom Train).*

1975   The film *Guérnica* released. Visits Tokyo where his work is performed at the No Theater.

1976   *The Architect and the Emperor of Assyria,* staged at La Mama in New York under the direction of Tom O'Horgan, receives a rave review from Clive Barnes in *The New York Times* of May 30, 1976.

1977   *The Architect* is performed in Barcelona in April. Arrabal declines to return to his native Spain, however, until all political prisoners are released.

CHAPTER 1

Biography

E VERY writer puts something of himself, his experiences, dreams and obsessions into his work. The degree to which the reader's knowledge of an author's personal world enhances his understanding and appreciation of that writer's work, however, varies substantially. Fernando Arrabal must be counted among those authors whose immersion into their own work has been most insistent and pervasive. For that reason, a familiarity with the events which affected him most strongly and with the various forces which helped to shape his thought processes and produce his concept of art and aesthetics is of paramount importance to the interpretation of his diverse literary production.

The early years of Arrabal's life were so traumatic in nature and left such a deep imprint on the young man's psyche that much of his writing, even into the 1960s, was constituted, in part, of psychological exercises directed toward the resolution of deep-seated conflicts and anxieties. As Arrabal himself has commented: "I believe that I have a right to be a writer: that of possessing a biography rich in bizarre phenomena, in striking events."[1] The repressive character of Arrabal's formative years was so marked that the liberating nature of many of his subsequent experiences, both personal and intellectual, had an extraordinary impact on him, which resonated throughout his artistic productions. The energy, *joie de vivre,* intellectual curiosity and political *engagement* of this author today are so intense that, given the international character of his present existence, they assure the continued growth of his vision and his art.

I *The Early Years*

Fernando Arrabal was born in Melilla, Spanish Morocco, on August 11, 1932. His older sister, Mari-Carmen, was born the previous year, while the family was still in Spain, and the birth of his brother, Julio, followed two years after his own. The young Fernando's only memory of the four years spent in Melilla and, concomitantly, of his father, Fernando Arrabal Ruiz, is of the latter's hands as they gently covered his son's legs with sand at the beach.[2] The relative peace and harmony of those early years as reflected in that image was abruptly shattered on July 17, 1936, when the Civil War broke out in Morocco, and Arrabal's father, a leftist, was dragged from bed, arrested and summarily sentenced to death.[3] Arrabal was never to see him again; his mother refused to permit her incarcerated husband to receive his children and to bid them farewell because she considered anyone of his political persuasions unworthy to do so.[4] For the next thirteen years, his father's memory was purposely eradicated from the family; even his physical image was systematically excised from all accessible photographs.

Soon after the arrest and imprisonment of his father, Arrabal's family moved to Ciudad Rodrigo,[5] a small Spanish city north of Portugal, where they joined his maternal grandparents. The four years spent in that city are documented, in fictional form, in his novel *Baal Babylone* (1959). The young boy was subjected to the traditional pressures of a dogmatic Catholic upbringing and to the demands placed on all young Spanish males to develop traits associated with masculinity. After the death of his grandfather, the family moved to Madrid where the young Arrabal resumed his education under the Escolapian Order at the San Anton School.

Self-doubt, insecurities, and complexes, associated in part with his small stature and large head,[6] emerged in the repressive atmosphere that permeated post-Civil War Spain. The cruelty of his teachers and fellow students,[7] the harshness of his religious training and of the forms of penitence practiced, and the hatred and mistrust evidenced by the lingering retributions against supporters of the Republic had a profound effect on the sensitive boy; but the instinct of rebellion had not yet developed. Arrabal remained for the moment unswerving in his religious faith and his devotion to his mother. Like other Spanish dramatists,[8] his nascent talent for the theater found an outlet in performances presented for his mother with his toy stage.

Resistance began to manifest itself after his enrollment in a Military Academy in 1947. At about that time, he was introduced to the films of Charlie Chaplin, Laurel and Hardy, and others, as well as to the imaginative fantasies of the writer Lewis Carroll; he found these much more to his liking than his studies. The strength for full-fledged rebellion, however, came from a chance discovery. In 1949, Arrabal happened upon a collection of his father's letters and photographs hidden in a trunk in the attic. The impact of that discovery on the young man was tremendous. As a result of his realization of what his mother had done,[9] he ceased speaking to her, maintaining his silence for five years, a period of intense psychological turmoil in which Arrabal made great strides toward psychic and intellectual maturity.

II *Adolescence and Maturity*

During his years of self-imposed silence, Arrabal was taunted by the other members of his family who mockingly referred to him as the "poet." The situation at home became untenable for everyone; Arrabal was sent to a trade school in Tolosa where he studied the paper industry at an institution run by the same religious order (the Escolapians) as his first school in Madrid. There he began to develop the tuberculosis that was to plague him throughout his early twenties. Upon returning to Madrid, he began to study law at the same time that he held a job in industry.[10] During this period, Arrabal's intellectual horizons expanded rapidly. He spent countless hours reading at the Ateneo in Madrid, where the authors "discovered" included two whose writings were to inspire and profoundly affect his own work, and who continue to fascinate and influence him even today: Franz Kafka and Fyodor Dostoievsky.

In 1952 Arrabal wrote what was to be his first published play: *Los soldados (The Soldiers).*[11] It was not, however, his first endeavor in the realm of theater. Since childhood, Arrabal had been attracted to that genre; countless "manuscripts" of a less formal nature had been the product of his early years. The satisfaction derived from the publication of his play gave impetus to his literary career; in 1953 his drama, *Los hombres del triciclo (The Men of the Tricycle),* received the second prize in a contest held in Barcelona. It was considered for the top award, but one judge objected that it had borrowed too heavily from Beckett. This perplexed the young author, who had never heard of that writer and thought that the judge had said Bécquer. Arrabal could not understand how his work related to that of the nineteenth-century Spanish Romantic poet, Gustavo Adolfo Bécquer.

Arrabal's knowledge of the contemporary theater expanded

rapidly during the following years. In 1954 he made his first trip to France, hitchhiking to Paris where he attended a performance of Bertold Brecht's *Mother Courage* given by the Berlin Ensemble. In the summer of that year, Arrabal, after returning to Spain, met Luce Moreau, a young French student of Spanish literature. His psychological background — reflective of his sheltered existence, female dominated homelife, and personal insecurities — produced a great deal of anxiety in the initial stages of his relationship with her. Some of his feelings found expression in the play, *Fando and Lis,* written in 1955. But his sentiments of love also complemented his growing artistic ambitions.[12] During that same year Arrabal received his introduction to the theater of Samuel Beckett and of Eugène Ionesco, attending performances of their plays. He returned to France in December, 1955, on a government grant to study theater. His plans had to be revised completely, however, when he became extremely ill with tuberculosis. Much of 1956 saw him confined to a sanatorium (at Bouffemont); he underwent surgery in November of that year. His confinement had its positive aspects, however. The long hours of forced physical inactivity were filled with reading, thinking and writing. It proved to be a highly productive period in his life. A corollary interest was also developed during this time: chess. It has remained a consuming passion until the present time.[13]

The following year, 1957, was marked by a major professional breakthrough; with the assistance of Geneviève Serreau, Arrabal obtained a contract for the publication of his works with Julliard that guaranteed him a fixed monthly income. During the following year, his play, *The Men of the Tricycle,* became the first of his works to be professionally performed. It was presented in Madrid on January 29, 1958, at the Teatro de Bellas Artes by the Dido Pequeño Theater Company under the direction of Josefina Sánchez Pedreño. Two days later, Arrabal was married to Luce Moreau. His personal and professional life had emerged from the nightmare of his childhood traumas; although some of the latter continued to haunt his dreams and his plays, the possibilities for continued progress toward artistic maturity and public recognition seemed excellent.

III *Artistic Maturity and International Renown*

A lull in Arrabal's dramatic production occurred during the

years 1959-1962. However, during that period, productions of his plays were mounted in several countries.[14] He began to experiment with other literary genres; his first novel, *Baal Babylone,* was completed in 1959. Moreover, Arrabal obtained a Ford Foundation grant to visit the United States, initiating what has proven to be a continuing passion for world travel. During his sojourn in New York City, he followed the tradition established by his fellow dramatist, Federico García Lorca, residing for a period of time in John Jay Hall at Columbia University. His travels throughout North America and Cuba were structured around his interest in examining the work of various experimental theater groups. The trip proved stimulating despite his disillusionment with the state of experimental theater at that time in the United States.

Arrabal's literary career entered a totally new phase in 1962. His contact with André Breton and the Surrealists and his association with the writers who, in collaboration with Arrabal originated the Panic Movement,[15] all provided him with the stimulation needed to resume writing for the theater with renewed vigor. His works began to be performed in Paris with increasing regularity; although often received by the critics with overt hostility, he began, nevertheless, to acquire something of a following.[16] Arrabal also continued to seek new modes of artistic expression. Judging himself incapable of mastering the technical challenges posed by painting, he refused to deny himself the opportunity of utilizing that medium; he began to collaborate with several artists who produced canvases for him according to his specifications.[17] These diverse associations and experiences helped to facilitate his maturation as an artist. In 1965 he wrote *L'Architecte et L'Empereur d'Assyrie (The Architect and the Emperor of Assyria),* a long, complex work considered by many critics to be his masterpiece.

The increased exposure received by Arrabal's plays facilitated the expansion of his artistic contacts; during the mid-sixties he met and began to collaborate with Victor García, Jérôme Savary and Jorge Lavelli, the three expatriated Argentine directors whose staging of his work has been most satisfying to Arrabal. Some critics continued to denigrate the playwright and his work, filling their reviews with expressions of outrage and disgust, but others, equally respected, began to accept what he was doing, praising unabashedly both the productions of his works and the plays themselves. By the late 1960s, Arrabal was well on the way to becoming the most performed playwright in Paris. If the "success" of an avant-garde writer is directly related to the controversy surrounding him and his work, the attention that Arrabal was receiving during this period reached sufficient proportions to assure him a position of prominence among writers of experimental theater.

IV *Political Commitment*

Arrabal's works have always embodied a political dimension. His own postwar experiences and psychological traumas found expression in his plays, providing an intense, highly personal view of Spain, strongly critical of totalitarian oppression and the institutions that served it. Despite the juvenile perspective of his earlier works and the subjectivity of their *Weltanschauung,* the very nature of the material allowed for a transcendence of purely national concerns and an incorporation of genuine universality. The author's perspective on politics and his approach to the identification and denunciation of political tyranny broadened tremendously as a result of several personal experiences during the late 1960s.

While visiting Spain in 1967, Arrabal, during a public appearance in a department store, was asked to autograph a copy of *Arrabal celebrando la ceremonia de la confusión (Arrabal Celebrating the Ceremony of Confusion)* with a "Panic" inscription. He wrote the following: "Me cago en Dios, en la patria y en todo lo demás" ("I shit on God, my country and everything else"). The statement was read by a loyal supporter of the Franco regime; and on July 21, 1967, Arrabal was arrested in the middle of the night, held incommunicado in a subterranean cell without access to an attorney, and then imprisoned at Carabanchel to await trial.[18] Fortunately for the author, the Spanish government had not been fully cognizant of the reputation he had attained among avant-garde writers. Letters began to deluge the Spanish embassies from such luminaries of the world of letters as Peter Weiss, Samuel Beckett, Eugène Ionesco, Jean Anouilh, and others. Under that pressure, the Spanish government deemed it prudent to find a satisfactory means of acquitting Arrabal. It was decided that he had written "Patra," referring to his cat Cleopatra, and not "Patria" (country).[19] His blasphemy was also excused by the court on the grounds that the drinks of aniseed and stimulant pills taken to counteract his nervousness before appearing at the department

store had left him in a state in which he could not be held account-
able for his actions.

His stay in Spainsh prisons lasted from July 21 until August 14.
In addition to reviving his tuberculosis and exposing him to the horrors of the Spanish penal system and the plight of its victims, the
experience aroused in him a renewed identification with his father.
As he himself has stated: "There, in that hole, I reentered my
mother's womb. I was in the darkness, isolated, outside of everything, and I was born a second time. I reexperienced all the pain of
birth ... It seemed as if I was being born into the real world of
injustice, torture and intolerance. A world that had been absent
until then from my life and my work ... And I asked myself if it
was not a means of retrieving my true childhood, hidden in forget-
fulness, of drawing nearer to my father."[20] The experience aroused
such indignation in him, especially in light of his contact with fellow "political" prisoners, many of whom had been immured for
years for rather nebulous offenses,[21] that shortly after his release he
presented their situation in an article written for the French news-
paper, *Le Monde*. The nightmares that plagued him as a direct
result of his incarceration provided new inspiration for images and
even entire works.

Less than a year after his experience in Spanish prisons, Arrabal
was once again directly involved in an event that had strong political overtones; he participated in the student uprisings of May,
1968, in Paris. His artistic response to the fervor aroused there took
the form of several works of guerrilla theater, the most immediate
and direct sub-genre of political drama. That experience made him
more deeply aware of the universal nature of political oppression
and rendered him more sensitive to its machinations, more fully
committed to its opposition.

Arrabal's artistic endeavors have continued to expand in scope.
He directed a major production of one of his own plays for the first
time in 1969 (*Et ils passèrent des menottes aux fleurs — And They
Put Handcuffs on the Flowers*) — premiered at the Théâtre de
l'Epée de Bois in Paris on September 26.[22] The following year, he
wrote and directed his first film, *Viva la muerte (Long Live Death)*,
shot in Tunisia. The 1970s have been active, satisfying years for
Arrabal. He has gained increased acceptance from drama critics,[23]
produced two more films and authored many more plays; and during these years he and his wife became the parents of two children.
His inclination for travel has taken him to all parts of the world,

from Latin America to Japan. He has become the object of exhaustive study by scholars from a number of different countries[24] and has received extensive publicity in the media, bringing his extravagances, obsessions, and artistic achievements to the attention of an ever widening audience. Despite this expanded exposure, the controversial nature of his work has remained unchanged. As Charles Marowitz has so perceptively stated: "Arrabal is in his true element at the burning center of controversy."[25] At the relatively young age of forty-six, Fernando Arrabal has already produced a large body of work;[26] his energy and inventiveness seem to assure continued innovations in form and technique as he seeks to give expression to those concerns, both constant and new which dominate his thoughts and dreams.

V   Arrabal: The Man and the Writer

In the study that provides the most direct and complete access to Arrabal as a person as well as an artist, the *Entretiens avec Arrabal (Interviews with Arrabal),* his interviewer, Alain Schifres, comments that for Arrabal theater is life itself, and life consists of a never ending series of "coups de théâtre."[27] The inseparability of life and theater becomes a living reality in the presence of the dramatist. He is capable of all types of behavioral extravagances and seems to take especial delight in baiting and outraging audiences, both inside and outside the theater. And yet, as one comes to know Arrabal personally, it is evident that this iconoclastic comportment is by no means a genuine expression of his inner feelings about himself or of his true relationship to the world around him. To a large extent, Arrabal seems still to be compensating for deep-seated insecurities and self-doubt. But he is not unwilling to confess that the image of himself that he often seeks to project is a false one. As he himself says to Schifres: "One is inclined to think that Arrabal, who is so frequently characterized as the 'pornographic writer,' the 'sexually obsessed artist,' must lead a scandalous life. In fact, quite the opposite is true. If there are any orgies in Paris, I am the last to know about them and the last to participate in them."[28]

The same wit that is so evident in Arrabal's theater is frequently experienced by those in personal contact with him.[29] He exudes energy, humor, and *joie de vivre;* once his more abrasive actions and "obscene" comments can be viewed in their proper perspective, he emerges as a thoroughly likeable individual. However, the brilliance of his wit, as well as his zest for life, constitute only one facet of his complex, often paradoxical personality. In a manner similar to that of his fellow playwright, Federico García Lorca,[30] Arrabal has his dark side. He communicates this other dimension of his psychological makeup in a moving statement made to Alain Schifres: "There are moments in my life when I am tempted to go to sleep. As I have difficulty falling asleep, I think, with my eyes open in the darkness, and they become moments of horrifying lucidity. It is the time in my life where I feel the most lucid, it is the instant when I see clearly and irrevocably that my life is a horrible farce, and that I am condemned to suffer and to remain ignorant. And in those moments, I am convinced that in an hour I will commit suicide."[31]

Although Arrabal has gradually expanded the artistic media in which he seeks to give expression to the whole range of his thoughts and concerns, the theater remains the genre with which he wishes to be most closely associated. He finds inspiration for his work primarily in his own dreams and experiences; the initial stimuli are generally highly visual in nature.[32]

There is a definite pattern to Arrabal's work habits. He is a late riser; his most productive periods of the day are the afternoon and evening. With the exception of his dreams, which he often transcribes upon arising and utilizes in creating plays, he prefers to work without notes. The creative act is almost a mystical event for Arrabal. He sees himself as a medium for outside forces; his dreams, and ultimately his characters as well, control him. He explains the process of writing as follows:

> When I write, I am in an abnormal situation, shut into my room, smoking my pipe, with a special atmosphere around me, and I'm not what you would call normal. I start to live intensely. I think, and every page I write provokes emotions in me. I think the writer's procedure is very much like that of a man who sets himself a chess problem. There is confusion and there are chess pieces. He doesn't know what he's going to do and then suddenly there's a spark. The problem has been invented. I don't know what's going to happen next. I let my characters surprise me.[33]

For Arrabal, writing must constitute a response to a challenge, hence the analogy with a chess problem. He feels that he writes most spontaneously when things have been going badly, when he is at odds with himself or with external reality.[34]

Arrabal's earlier works are generally written in Spanish, then translated into French with the assistance of his wife, for the purposes of publication. In more recent years, as his French has become more facile, he has occasionally written first drafts in French, correcting his initial efforts later. (Spanish still remains the primary language for first drafts, however.)[35] The tension between his native Spanish sensibility and his love for his adopted city, Paris, between his rejection of his mother and his country — and the attraction that they both exert upon him, and the struggle between his public personality and his private fears and anxieties all contribute to the complexity and fascination of Arrabal. The paradoxes and antimonies which characterize the playwright's personality are all reflected in his plays in a manner that elucidates the pivotal relationship between the author's life and his works.

CHAPTER 2

The Early Plays

A S a young writer Fernando Arrabal was largely unaware of literary movements such as Surrealism and of the seminal works of luminaries of the contemporary theater including Samuel Beckett, Eugène Ionesco, Antonin Artaud and Jean Genet; but his earliest plays intuitively assimilated certain features associated with those writers and their work. His assiduous denial of overt influence confirms the observations of many astute literary critics; writers generally do not borrow directly from one another, but develop their thematic and aesthetic paradigms in response to mutually shared socio-political forces dominating their epoch. It is the critic who must search for and identify the features commonly present in the works of a particular group of writers; in certain cases, the name generally used to describe a given literary style or philosophy originated with a critic rather than with one of the writers categorized.[1] In seeking first to establish the character of Arrabal's early plays, and later to examine the manner in which his technique evolves, it will be helpful to utilize the widely accepted nomenclature associated with the contemporary stage in order to identify and analyze the salient features of his theater.

The characteristic most closely associated with the first phase of Arrabal's dramatic production is his penchant for childlike characters who seem totally oblivious to the moral implications of their actions, whether tender and loving or cruel and sadistic. His preference for a juvenile perspective may be explainable in part by his need to return to the innocence of childhood in order to deal psychologically with traumas suffered in his own youth. Stylistically, the resultant clash between the lyrical quality and ingenuous tone of the dialogue — and the violence and cruelty of the action — produces a pervasive dramatic tension. As Martin Esslin has observed, the conflation of poetry and cruelty, of spontaneous tenderness and destructiveness, is a significant component of the Theater of the Absurd.[2]

In evoking the subconscious realm where opposites can coexist and ultimately be reconciled, Arrabal's theater also suggests the Surrealist vision. Although the tenets of Surrealism as a formal artistic movement receive fuller expression in Arrabal's "Panic" period, his early plays already contain a childlike language[3] free of stifling linguistic patterns; this style corresponds to the writer's surreal vision, reflecting his abrogation of "adult" constraints on both thought and action.[4] Arrabal has always linked dreams with artistic creation;[5] this additional manifestation of Surrealism in his theater also expresses his view that the real and imaginary worlds are inseparable components of the schizophrenic vision that dominates the twentieth century.[6] Consequently, many early plays already exhibit to a degree the oneiric atmosphere that will later subsume the artistic milieu of his theater.

Surrealism, the Absurd, and the avant-garde as a whole all derive, at least tangentially, from Romanticism, embodying both its *angst* and note of rebellion. The title of Robert Brustein's book on the contemporary drama, *The Theater of Revolt,* supports this view, alluding to both the genesis and the intent of the works considered. Many of Brustein's observations, especially with respect to Artaud and Genet, also provide insight into the works of Arrabal; the following general statement could have been inspired by Arrabal's example: "The theater of revolt, in other words, is extremely self-conscious and self-involved, as befits a Romantic movement. And like the other Romantics, the dramatist begins to enter his work to a hitherto unprecedented degree."[7]

In a manner similar to that of August Strindberg, Arrabal's early theater serves as a forum through which he can externalize and hopefully resolve his innermost psychological traumas. Some of his plays derive their basic structure from the building and releasing of psychic tension, a device which confirms their therapeutic nature. This component, often dominant in the early plays, encourages a biographical and psychological approach by the critic. The dreamlike atmosphere suggestive of the author's subconscious mind is projected on stage in order to identify and exorcise the suppressed forces encountered therein.[8] Yet even his early endeavors also manage to transcend the purely subjective and to make a meaningful statement about the human condition.

The dominant figure in the subconscious of the author and concomitantly, in his theater, is the mother. Her role in his plays (particularly in those of his first period, but also in his Panic works) is an incisive one. As Phyllis Boring has established, the mother comes to incarnate the worst features of Spanish totalitarian oppression and of the church that served it.[9] Yet Arrabal finds it far from easy to overcome her allure for him or to reject her totally and unequivocally. The psychological conflicts generated by his relationship with that parent provide much of the tension of these early dramas. According to Jungian psychology, man has a natural tendency to project an *anima* derived from the mother on other women; accordingly, the female characters in these plays embody conflicting 'forces which exacerbate the strained relationship between themselves and the male protagonists (Arrabal's counterparts).

Raymond-Mundschau has utilized this recurrent situation to illuminate the structure of these plays; she schematizes the relationship of the characters to one another and to the world in the form of a triangle. The female, who can be either the oppressor or the oppressed, becomes the intermediary force between the hero (who is at once good and cruel, innocent and guilty, slave and master) and the outside adult world, typically repressive and incomprehensible.[10] José Polo de Bernabé, in his analysis of her schema, notes that this tripartite structure also reflects a fundamental relationship governing all of theater: that of protagonist, antagonist and audience.[11] Thus, both within the world of the play itself and in the broader context of the theatrical production or *mise-en-scène,* the groundwork has been laid for what Arrabal will later develop into an expansive view of theater which takes as its point of departure a relationship between characters, but ultimately embraces the audience as well in a total theater experience.[12]

Humor is another constant in Arrabal's theater figuring prominently in his early plays and continuing to expand in function and form as his artistic technique evolves. His use of humor is consonant with his psychological focus and concomitant fixation upon a childlike perspective. As Sigmund Freud explains in his analysis of the union of wit and the unconscious, "humor can now be conceived as the loftiest of defense functions... It is even credible that it is again the connection with the infantile that puts at humor's disposal the means for this function."[13] The defensive nature of Arrabal's humor has been noted by a number of critics. There is an intense identification of author and character; hence, laughter within his theater functions as a highly personal means for the play-wright to deal with his concerns: "And he is afraid. And he acts like children when they are afraid (like Chaplin), he laughs: both to *humor* the ferocious creatures and to escape his own fear."[14]

Much of Arrabal's comic inspiration is of the sort generally known as "black humor,"[15] an integral component of the gro-tesque, a mode found in Arrabal's earliest works, which is enriched and expanded later. By transforming death, violence and cruelty into something comical and consequently insignificant, Arrabal seeks to liberate himself from the chaos and horror of both his inner world and of external reality, realms which may merge into a virtually inseparable whole. Gloria Orenstein elucidates the intent and effect of black humor, providing insight into Arrabal's theater when she states: "Black humor, then, is the supreme method of dis-orienting, dislocating and confusing the senses so that a pleasurable and humorous response will be the reaction to the perception of a tragic reality and so that an aesthetic pleasure will be derived from the spectacle of cruelty or sadism."[16]

The union of horror and laughter, an essential component of the grotesque, is also associated with the Theater of the Absurd.[17] The growth of Arrabal as a dramatist can be documented, in part, by studying the change in the nature of the humor he employs in his theater. In its earliest phase, the humor in his plays is primarily lin-guistic, deriving from the naiveté of his childlike characters. The earliest plays reveal a dominant influence: the nonsense humor of Lewis Carroll's *Alice in Wonderland* and *Through the Looking Glass*. As Arrabal enriches his technique, his humor becomes more visual, more baroque and, ultimately, more multifaceted in scope.

Another important constant in Arrabal's theater that begins to emerge during his first period and later develops into a central con-stituent of his work is a circularity of structure, echoed in his sym-bolic use of the wheel, and the balloon and in his predilection for the labyrinth. This feature is also aligned with the tradition of the Absurd.[18] The efficacy of this design, which can be identified with the *ouroboros* (the serpent that bites its tail), has been noted by Alain Schifres; he discusses Arrabal's use of tautologies, his obses-sive repetition of situations and dramatic effects, and the metamor-phosis and ambivalence of characters, relating them to the author's view of theater as ceremony.[19] This tendency encourages an arch-typal analysis of these plays. As Northrop Frye has demonstrated, in its archetypal phase, the poem (work of literature) imitates nature as a cyclical process, emphasizing patterns and rhythms of recurrence in ritual and dream[20] — two key components of Arrabal's theater.

In the dream-like atmosphere of many of Arrabal's early plays, repetitions, cycles and ceremonies already play a significant role. Reality remains elusive, subjective and highly volatile. The characters' rapid changes reflect the instability and senselessness of the world as they and their "creator" see it. Life becomes a game without fixed rules, a puzzle without a concrete solution, a kaleidoscope of changing configurations and patterns. The playwright himself can be found at the center of that fascinating, threatening and elusive microcosmos carefully constructed to project his own personal vision of life. As Jung has stated, the man possessed by the *anima* (as the Arrabalian characters under the influence of the mother figure undoubtedly are) sees all of life as a game or puzzle.[21]

The *Weltanschauung* of the early plays is presented primarily from a juvenile perspective, encompassing a socio-political dimension frequently subordinated to their author's psychological fixations. Considered as a whole, these early plays contain features of the Theater of the Absurd and of Surrealism without really falling under either rubric. The personal involvement of the author is paramount throughout, as is his penchant for dark humor, games, circles, metamorphoses of characters and recurring motifs and events. Paradoxes abound; the lyrical is united with the cruel, humor is combined with terror, innocence with depravity, existential anguish assimilates frivolous jocularity, and love and hatred coalesce. These conflicting forces which seek hope and release from life's constraints through their resolution provide structure and dramatic tension in many of Arrabal's plays.

This basic polarity in its broadest sense has been defined as destruction (alienation and repression) and creation (art) by José Ortega.[22] In his first plays, highly subjective, psychological tensions resonate with both national and metaphysical concerns as the young Arrabal utilizes his theater to attempt to resolve his own anxieties as well as to communicate artistically universal joys, fears and frustrations. His first play, *Los soldados (Picnic on the Battlefield),* focuses more objectively on sociological issues than do many subsequent works of the dramatist's pre-1960 theater.

I   Los soldados (Picnic on the Battlefield)

Picnic on the Battlefield (1952) is a paragon of simplicity that utilizes the clash between the horror of objective reality and the naiveté of the characters, reflected by their insouciant dialogue, to generate humor and dramatic tension. The incongruous nature of the piece is captured in its central situation as communicated by the English title. Zapo, a soldier, is visited by his parents during a lull between battles. They bring supplies for a picnic, spreading their blanket and indulging themselves right in the midst of war. They are briefly interrupted by the appearance of Zepo, an enemy soldier. After his "capture," he is invited to join the picnic. Zapo's parents see only the romantic side of war; his father laments the abasement of the ceremonious aspect of battle resulting from the elimination of horses and of much of the pomp and splendor of warfare. Several stretcherbearers appear and express their dismay at the scarcity of dead and wounded. The picnic reaches its height of festiveness as a *pasodoble* is played on a phonograph. The gaiety of the scene ends abruptly when the participants are suddenly felled by machine-gun fire.

In *Picnic on the Battlefield,* Arrabal remained largely detached from the work; personal identification with characters and the dramatic situation is virtually nonexistent. Yet even in this didactic piece, inspired by the Korean War rather than by the author's own experience, there is an autobiographical note. Zapo's mother, Madame Tepan, mirrors Arrabal's own mother both in name (Teran) and in her blind admiration for the military uniform and its aura. She is the epitome of superficiality in her mannerisms and concerns. Thus the ironic parody of the play as a whole is reflected in the realm of the personal, linking the absurdity of the institution of war with that of Arrabal's own intimate environment.

Arrabal's farcical treatment seeks to render the idea of war totally ludicrous. The principal weapon in his artistic arsenal is humor which in this work relies heavily on the construction of incongruities. The idea of a picnic on the battlefield provides the basis, reinforced by numerous nonsensities. Mme. Tepan's preoccupation with decorum is one example; she refuses to allow her son to bring his rifle to the table and seems to be more concerned with his personal hygiene than with his genuine well-being. Some of the humor reflects Arrabal's interest in the music hall and in silent film, important influences on the Theater of the Absurd. Examples include: Zapo and Zepo's mutual terror when they first see one another (evidenced by their simultaneous raising of their hands in an attempt to surrender to one another); Zapo's knitting and Zepo's flower-making to while away the hours in the trenches; Mme. Tepan's use of an open umbrella to ward off bombs during an air raid; and her attempt to play a beret rather than a record on their phonograph.

Arrabal's specific debt to Lewis Carroll's *Alice in Wonderland* and *Through the Looking Glass* in this play has been convincingly demonstrated by Irmgard Anderson.[23] Zapo and Zepo, two soldiers who are virtually indistinguishable (affirming the brotherhood of man), are strongly aligned to Tweedledee and Tweedledum who view their fight as a game that provides an opportunity to dress up. Like Zepo and Zapo, they have no real understanding of why they are fighting. Tweedledee's use of an umbrella in their fight is echoed in Mme. Tepan's use of the same object to ward off bombs. The nonsense world of Alice utilized here by Arrabal portrays the equally illogical world of man; the only distinction between the two realms is that what is revealed finally as a child's dream in Carroll's delightful work emerges as an adult nightmare at the end of Arrabal's play.

The *jeu*, or game, a central motif throughout much of Arrabal's theater, plays a significant role in this first drama. Vocabulary and imagery used in the play equate war and its components with a broad range of playful competitions. The parents ask each soldier how they have been doing with their target practice; the targets are, of course, living human beings. Zapo theorizes that his parents were able to get to him because the soldiers assumed they were "referees." When Zapo "captures" Zepo, he does so by touching him as if they were playing tag. After the two soldiers reveal their total ignorance of war and the reason for their involvement in it, Mme. Tepan suggests that the solution might be for them to play together. The innocence and naiveté of the characters underscores the horror of war. Zapo and Zepo do not even know if hand grenades should be thrown backward or forward.[24] Their defense against their own incomprehension of war (and of life) is to make a game out of war; but this course of action is doomed to failure, as indicated by the play's conclusion. Despite the ingenuousness of the characters and the "nonsense" quality of some dialogue and actions, the attitude toward life and war which emerges is far more humane and "logical" than that of the establishment which utilizes war for its own ends.

Picnic on the Battlefield owes some of its impact to the utilization of the grotesque through the dehumanization of characters.

Zapo's parents encourage him to pose for a photograph with his foot on Zepo's stomach, as if the latter were a beast of prey. The stretcherbearers generate the darkest humor with their frustration at the absence of dead and wounded. It is this latter element which causes Arnold Heidsieck to state that the grotesque functions to strip away the veil of supposedly moral and political aims and to expose the "manufactured" deformation of man, the inhumanity perpetrated by men on other men.[25] Mme. Tepan's final observation, after the stretcherbearers have departed with the picknickers' assurance that they will help them in their search for more corpses, is illustrative of Arrabal's use of irony to add impact to his theme. She states: "That's what's so pleasant about spending a Sunday in the country. You always meet such nice people" (p. 121). By dehumanizing his characters, Arrabal succeeds in communicating the dehumanization effected by war on all human beings.

Picnic on the Battlefield contains absurd humor, incongruity, irony, grotesquerie and an overriding clash between tone and content which establishes it as a uniquely Arrabalian work with an identity of its own outside the norms of any one literary movement. Although Arrabal has repudiated the play to a large degree because of its didactic intent, it does, despite a somewhat superficial, obvious treatment of its theme, exhibit a talent for both verbal and visual stage humor. *El triciclo* (*The Tricycle,* 1953), a longer, more complex work, belongs more in the mainstream of Arrabal's dramatic production and displays a richer and more highly developed artistic vocabulary.

II   El triciclo (The Tricycle)

In comparison with *Picnic on the Battlefield, The Tricycle* demonstrates a charm, tenderness, lyricism, and verbal freedom which borders on the delirious and confirms Arrabal's promise as a writer of poetic theater. The plot is a model of simplicity. The play's trio of male characters — Apal, Climando, and the Old Man — are vagabonds living on the margin of modern bourgeois society. In their dramatic ambience, almost totally divorced from objective reality, Climando's principal activity involves an old box-tricycle which he uses to give rides to children in the park. He is in love with Mita, a childlike character with a more highly developed intuition of the nature of the world. They all suffer from a lack of food and

live in constant fear of hotel porters and policemen. Their desires
are small; Climando would like enough money to purchase the tricycle and to buy an anchovy sandwich for himself and each of his
friends. When a man from the "real" world begins to follow Mita,
showing her the money in his wallet, Climando thinks of taking it
so that they will be able to satisfy their needs. Apal tells them that
to do so they must kill the stranger. Mita bares her legs to attract
him, and Apal and Climando move to carry out their plan as the
first act concludes.

The second act of *The Tricycle* is basically actionless. The presence of the "cops" is confirmed early; from that point on the
characters are immobilized as they await the inevitable. The policemen speak in incomprehensible gibberish; genuine communication
between them and other characters proves impossible. At the conclusion, Climando and Apal turn over their possessions to their two
friends and go off to their death with the police as Mita and the Old
Man ride away together on the tricycle.

The symbol of the tricycle is central to both the play's theme and
structure. The circular shape of its wheels reflects the cyclical construction of the work; the tricycle gives impetus to the movement of
the piece in the first act, reappears at the beginning of the second
act, but then remains motionless until the very end of the play when
the circle both ends and begins again as Mita and the Old Man
depart. The box on the tricycle is decorated with various characters
from *Alice in Wonderland* which help to reflect the childlike world
of which Mita and the male trio are representative. Much dramatic
tension emanates from the clash between the innocent, naive, fantasy world of the principal characters and the oppressive, frightening and incomprehensible nature of the "real" world. Climando
and Mita attempt, simultaneously, to find meaning and logic on a
macrocosmic scale and to retreat, out of fear, into their own microcosm through nonsense games and verbal legerdemain. Descriptions suggest a neorealistic set which clashes with the dream-like
quality of the play, adding to the thematic and dramatic dichotomy
that dominates the work. The dialogue is rich in verbal nonsequi-
turs and nonsense words, as the emotions experienced by the
characters (ranging from love and empathy to sadness, boredom
and fear) receive a full, albeit abstract expression in the text.

Arrabal's characters exhibit an amorality and ingenuousness in
these early plays that separates them from the hypocrisy and greed
of the outside world. They are reminiscent of Charlie Chaplin in

their gentleness, innocence and pride in their meager successes. As Jacques Guicharnaud states: "They love and betray what they love with the same innocence. They are often cowards, but have spurts of dignity. They are always bewildered by the world, sometimes manage to cheat it, but instead of happily or doubtfully going off into the sunset, they end by being crushed in some frightful way."[26] The tone of their language clashes with the horror of their worst deeds, introducing a note of pathos when they fall victim to the machinations of organized society. Climando and Mita's fascination with excretion and their focus on the simple, basic pleasures of life evinces the juvenile perspective of the play. But Apal, whose method of dealing with the horror of the macrocosmos surrounding their fantasy world is to sleep eighteen hours a day, is conscious of "the ways of the world." It is he who tells the others that they must kill the man with the banknotes, and it is also he who informs them that the cops have come to kill Climando and himself. There is a note of existential anguish about Apal, undeveloped since he chooses to escape from existence instead of coming to grips with it.

The man who is murdered and the police are representatives of an unfeeling, kafkaesque world of corruption and greed. Mita affirms a pure and simple life, rejecting the money of the man and the use to which he puts it. However, it is the failure of Climando and Apal to keep the two spheres totally separate which causes the crime and results in the destruction of these two characters. The nonfeeling policeman reveals his emotional emptiness by interrupting Climando and Mita at the moment they are about to kiss. Climando, on the other hand, affirms his basic kindness at the end of the play by purposely losing (for the first time) the nonsense game of logic which he periodically plays with the Old Man and by distributing his possessions among his friends. *The Tricycle* is a tender, humane evocation of the simple, childlike existence of man, threatened and ultimately destroyed by societal institutions which have become dehumanized, oppressive and senseless.

III   Fando y Lis (Fando and Lis)

Begun in Spain in 1955 and completed in Paris the following year, *Fando and Lis* is the first of Arrabal's plays utilized by the author to examine artistically his own psychological state. Much pathos derives from the intensity of the emotions and frustrations experienced by its male protagonist, a purposely undisguised counterpart of the author.[27] For the first time, the relationship between the characters becomes the central tension producing device in the drama. The characters as individuals are less important than is the dialectical nature of their relationship. Their thoughts and actions provide insight into the subconscious mind of the author, acquiring additional meaning in the context of the socio-political forces then dominant in Spain.

Like *The Tricycle, Fando and Lis* presents the conflict between the juvenile world of the protagonists and objective reality, represented by a mysterious trio of male characters. The main plot derives its structure from the periodic, irrational outbursts of sadism on the part of Fando — subtly induced by Lis herself who, although paralyzed, is really the stronger of the two. The cruelties culminate in the death of Lis at the hands of Fando; she is beaten fatally after she accidentally breaks his toy drum. Interspersed with the scenes between the young lovers are Fando's encounters with the trio of male characters who, like he and Lis, are seeking to reach Tar. In the play's brief final scene, Fando keeps his promise, made at the opening of the play, to visit Lis' grave with a dog and a flower. The discussion among the three men concerning what has happened becomes confused and disoriented; their comments blend the action of *Fando and Lis, The Tricycle* and *The Car Cemetery* with events from Arrabal's life. At the conclusion, Fando departs with the men to continue his quest to reach Tar.

The structure of *Fando and Lis* is essentially circular in nature. The opening discussion of Lis' death becomes the reality of the play's climax; Fando's promise in the first scene to visit Lis' grave is fulfilled in the final scene. The repeated departures of the characters toward Tar produce no genuine progress; they continually find themselves at the same starting point.[28] In one sense, the play reflects man's inability and specifically that of the author-protagonist to move toward objectives. The separation of the juvenile fantasy world of Fando and Lis from the abstract, incoherent realm of the three men also heightens dramatic contrast. The first and fourth scenes belong totally to the "young lovers." In the other three scenes, where the three men are present, Fando and Lis' relationship, in both its positive and negative aspects, becomes inoperative. The intensification of cruelty in Fando's treatment of Lis gives a linear structure to their two scenes, but within the broader context, all feeling of progress is lost. Fando has no concept of time; Lis suggests the possibility of her death in the first scene and controls Fando's actions by anticipating what will happen. Fando's perspective is limited to an eternal, inescapable present; although he joins the others at the end of the play, he remains alienated both from himself and the world.

Fando and Lis can be viewed as a presentation of Arrabal's own psychic state at the time of the play's composition. His new-found love for Luce Moreau caused him a great deal of pain because of his traumatic childhood and lingering self-doubts. It is almost as though Lis were addressing Arrabal himself when she says that the one thing Fando can do for her is to "stand up for yourself in life."[29] Lis' paralysis, in Jungian terms, denotes Fando's projection upon her of an *anima* strongly reflective of his mother's influence on him; and it is this psychic "paralysis" that precludes Fando's fulfilling the love that he feels.[30] Fando's feelings of guilt alternating with his mistreatment of Lis reflect Arrabal's repressed desire to kill his mother and are a reaction against the feelings of inadequacy which she has instilled.

Lis appears to be aware, on a subconscious level, of Fando's psychic state; she utilizes her intuitive knowledge to manipulate his actions, invoking progressively more violent sadistic acts from him eventually culminating in her death. Arrabal may be examining a significant component of all eroticism; his often cited comments about the violent nature of love and the sado-masochistic component of sexuality especially pervasive in Spain[31] lend credence to that interpretation. But Fando emerges as a pathetic, defeated figure at the play's conclusion, having failed to free himself from his stultifying attachment to the unseen, archetypal, devouring mother whose presence is implicit throughout the play.

Fando and Lis belong to the group of childlike characters populating so many of Arrabal's early plays. Their puerility manifests itself in a number of ways. Fando's joy in exhibiting the physical charms of Lis evokes a child's excitement at receiving and sharing a toy. Fando can also be extremely possessive of his "plaything," as evidenced by his use of a chain to attach Lis to her carriage. Lis is also capable of an immature sort of cruelty; in the second scene, she refuses to talk to Fando. A dialectical quality derives from the master-slave relationship of the young lovers, mirrored in the symbolic representation of the two realms they embody: the physical (Fando) and the mental (Lis). As José Ortega has stated, the subjective and the social nature of the author-character are inseparable in Arrabal's works.[32] Fando's psychological immaturity reflects his socio-political milieu which continues to influence the dramatic world of Arrabal's characters.

The seemingly unattainable solution to Fando's psychic impasse appears to reside in the mysterious Tar that he and the other characters strive vainly to reach. The exact nature and significance of Tar remain perplexingly elusive. Arrabal suggests that it may simply represent daily happiness or bourgeois comfort.[33] For Frances Greenbaum it becomes a symbol and synthesis for a multitude of human aspirations, especially knowledge and wisdom.[34] While there can be no simple, clear-cut answer, the most interesting observations concerning the nature of Tar are contained in Gloria Orenstein's study of the theater of the marvelous. She suggests that it is an anagram of the word "art";[35] her analysis of Arrabal's theater in the light of alchemical principles concentrates on his "Panic" period. But her observation that Tar represents the alchemical citadel where the individual is reintegrated into the whole and is unified with his archetype supports the overall theme of *Fando and Lis* extremely well. Fando's striving for psychic wholeness in order to be able to realize a mature love and to establish a place in the adult world fails; he is unable to progress at all toward Tar. Fando's quest reflects that of the author's; in seeking the resolution of his own psychic traumas through the juvenile dream world of his theater, Arrabal also places his hope in the mysterious Tar in its anagramatic form: ART.

Arrabal likes to refer to *Fando and Lis* as a contemporary *Romeo and Juliet*. Both plays deal with the tragic impossibility of love in their respective ambiences, but Fando's plight transcends the purely subjective to make a strong statement about the human condition. As Janet Díaz states in her perceptive study of Arrabal's theater: "The work is thoroughly existentialist in its expression of the need for the other, the absurdity of life and human activity, and the radical solitude and incommunication of the individual."[36]

IV   Cérémonie pour un Noir assassiné
(Ceremony for an Assassinated Black)

Ceremony for an Assassinated Black was written in 1956 while Arrabal was confined to a sanatorium at Bouffemont. It reflects the author's obsession with death which he burlesques and caricatures, seeking release from anguish through humor. The play demonstrates Arrabal's emerging concept of theater as ceremony (the title), utilizing the play within a play and a more sophisticated recourse to the grotesque in an attempt to explore more fully the possibilities of the stage.

The initial scene of the work introduces the childish vagabonds, Vincent and Jerome, who return to their squalid apartment with a trunk full of theater costumes and a fierce determination to become famous actors. Their childlike excitement at choosing roles and donning costumes is hardly tempered by the female voice heard periodically announcing the death of her father. They are joined by a black man, Francis of Assisi, a discophile, who is persuaded to take the role of Othello. Only he shows any concern for Luce, who has suffered the loss of her father. A burlesque reading of Othello's lines by Francis, in imitation of Jerome, is interrupted by the appearance of the girl at the scene's conclusion.

In the second scene, Vincent and Jerome expand their theater skills to stage design, utilizing the coffin of Luce's father as a medium for demonstrating their talents in that realm. To alleviate Luce's guilt over not crying at her father's funeral and to show that she is not really that wicked, they confess several murders they have committed.[37] A mock funeral procession with the corpse bedecked in the costume of Cyrano de Bergerac concludes the scene.

In the following scenes, Jerome and Vincent invite Luce to stay with them, presenting her with a flower and a light bulb (retaining the urinal because of its indispensability), and assure her that their relationship will remain chaste. Jerome, bored, soon expresses his desire to see her blood. Vincent decides that Luce's physical needs are not being met and persuades Francis to make love to her. When she leaves without saying goodbye, Vincent and Jerome conclude that Francis has alienated her affections, and they decide to murder him. After plunging a knife in his back, Jerome suffers a stroke.

The play's concluding scene takes place a week after the murder with the rotting cadaver causing complaints from the neighbors whose voices are heard offstage. With these periodic protestations in the background, Vincent and Jerome act out a scene from *Othello*. Luce props up Jerome and recites his lines for him, since his stroke has rendered him aphasic. As Vincent ecstatically proclaims the triumph that they will enjoy on the stage, the police finally break in.

Ceremony for an Assassinated Black (like *Fando and Lis* and *The Tricycle*) contains a trio of childlike male characters reminscent of the Marx Brothers; the black's reticence and love of music link him with Harpo. The names of the three male characters, taken from illustrious saints, are an immediate source of humor in light of the play's content and link religion and its ceremonies with the ritualistic quality of the play (a motif utilized to an even greater extent in subsequent works). The clash between the characters' ingenuousness and naiveté — which are basically endearing — and the horror of their deeds is more violent than in Arrabal's earlier plays. And the ferocity of his black humor reaches new heights of theatricality, particularly in the final scene.

The use of the theater motif throughout the play contributes to the ceremonious nature of the work, functioning to generate quintessential grotesque images. Death is ridiculed when Luce's deceased father is dressed as Cyrano de Bergerac in preparation for burial. And the reality of the odor emanating from a rotting corpse becomes a humorous tension producing device in the final scene as it elicits increasingly vigorous protests from the neighbors, culminating in the arrival of the police. Arrabal's sense of theater and penchant for dark humor combine to produce the hilarious yet horrifying scene in which *Othello* is performed by Vincent and a paralyzed Jerome, aided by Luce.

The spoof of traditional theater that is a byproduct of Vincent and Jerome's exercises in the theatrical arts may be viewed as a commentary on the state of traditional theater. *Ceremony for an Assassinated Black* constitutes both an attack on outmoded conventions and a demonstration of possibilities for a new liberated theater uniting humor, pathos, poetry and ritual in an innovative and meaningful way. Theater, as viewed by Arrabal, gives meaning to life. Luce is only able to cry in response to her father's death after Vincent and Jerome prepare the body "theatrically." The joy the characters experience at their rendition of *Othello* transcends the suggestion of doom introduced by the arrival of the police. Arrabal judges the play to be optimistic for that reason;[38] in light of his observation, the theme of the play may well be the efficacy of the theatrical ceremony as a means of combatting the anxieties and irrationalities plaguing man in today's world.

V   Le Labyrinthe (The Labyrinth)

Inspired by a nightmare he had while confined in the sanatorium at Bouffemont,[39] *The Labyrinth* (1956) is Arrabal's most kafkaesque play. Its focal point is its provocative central symbol: the

toilet to which Bruno and Etienne are chained at the beginning of
the work. Etienne manages to free himself, causing a great deal of
pain for Bruno who is sick and suffers from constant thirst. The
toilet is located in a clearing in the center of an immense maze of
blankets. Micaela enters the clearing and explains the origin of the
labyrinth and the nature of Justin's (her father) tyrannical rule over
her home and the surrounding land, including the labyrinth. Justin
himself enters the clearing and informs Etienne that he must stand
trial. While Justin is away looking for a judge, Bruno commits suicide, and Etienne and Micaela hide his body. After the Judge, a
farcical figure, arrives, a trial is conducted; and Etienne is sentenced to death. As the sound of drums draws nearer, Etienne des-
perately seeks to escape, but behind every blanket he finds a magically resuscitated Bruno blocking his way.

In the obsessive, delirious ambience of the play, which reflects
the turmoil of both Etienne's inner world and of external reality,
objective truth becomes elusive and subject to frequent, irrational
changes. Micaela initially seems to be a sweet, gentle, childlike
young woman. Yet in a later scene, she becomes a depraved
nymphomaniac and pathological liar, sexually assaulting Bruno
and contradicting everything that she had said previously. The
metamorphosis of characters reflects Etienne's inability to deal
with a devious, unstable world. And the contradictory qualities of
the characters symbolize the menacing aspects of life.

Metamorphoses, delirium, and nightmare, the principal elements
that produce the play's atmosphere, also complement the structure
of *The Labyrinth* and support the central role played by the metaphor of the maze. Micaela reveals that Bruno has had a series of
companions chained to him. Thus Bruno comes to represent the
obsessive, imprisoning component of man's subconscious while
Etienne's circular flight at the end of the play illustrates the eternal,
inescapable agony which imprisons modern man. The interminable
maze of blankets originated when the laundry accumulating in
Justin's basement threatened to overrun the house; the uncontrollable proliferation of the blankets exemplifies Ionesco's concept of
de trop. This irrational expansion of matter is an essential feature
of the Absurdists. Arrabal's vision of man trapped in a world
where everything is senselessly joined and menacingly crowded
exposes the totalitarian nature of political and psychological
forces. This feature of his theater, which receives a stronger expression in *The Labyrinth* than in any of Arrabal's previous plays is

associated with the grotesque mode, as Bert O. States has indicated: "Plays are not grotesque simply because they contain monsters and freakish events — but because the world of possible normalcy seems to have been engulfed, or is seriously threatened by some prodigious tendency to self-repetition and unbounded growth."[40]

Kafka's influence on Arrabal is manifest on both a political and metaphysical level in *The Labyrinth*. Etienne's plight is reminiscent of Joseph K's, and the courtroom scene in the play also links it with *The Trial*. Arrabal exposes the Kafkaesque bureaucracy and irrationality of "justice" in his play; he also introduces a note of grotesque parody by presenting the Judge as a coarse, farcical figure who crudely munches a sausage sandwich throughout the judicial proceedings. Several allusions are made in the play to the politics of Spain. Micaela's description of the atmosphere in Justin's house, where they must speak in whispers and are not allowed to look out of the windows, is strongly suggestive of Franco's Spain. And the Judge's admission that he is merely Justin's slave and is subject to his will reflects the reality of the political system in Spain under the Generalissimo; the judicial branch of the Spanish government enjoyed no real autonomy, but was subject to executive power, answerable ultimately to the dictator himself.

The psychological and the political merge in the figure of Bruno. Etienne is unable to escape from Bruno; Arrabal is "chained" to the obsessive elements of his own formative years. The chain that binds the two men together is equated, by one critic, with the umbilical cord.[41] Bruno's moans support this birth motif; although the chain is severed physically, Etienne cannot dismiss Bruno from his life (as Arrabal cannot forget his own father). Micaela's sexual advances to Bruno can then be viewed as depicting the frustration of man's Oedipal desires. The author's most personal psychic traumas resonate with the political and even the metaphysical in the imagery of the play. Etienne's plight is both Arrabal's in Spain and man's in the modern world.

As an introduction to *The Labyrinth,* Arrabal supplies a quote from the final chapter of Kafka's *Amerika* which refers to The Great Theater of Oklahoma. That Theater, which calls Karl Rossman today and today only in *Amerika,* adds another dimension to the play. Micaela's description of the superior order present in the seeming disorder of her father's rule alludes to the theater motif; it may be interpreted as a metaphor for the structure of Arrabal's

theater. Etienne's role is similar to Karl's in the Kafka novel. As
Heinz Politzer explains: "Whatever Kafka may have intended to
say here, whether this theater was to represent a judge of the dead,
a church, or an abstract court of truth, Karl is undoubtedly put into
a situation of being tested."[42] Kafka's mysterious Theater of Oklahoma and the irrevocable nature of the choice of joining or not
joining it become essential features of Arrabal's oneiric drama in
which Etienne's feelings of guilt and desires for liberation and fulfillment combine to produce frustration on the metaphysical level.
Like Karl, Etienne (and man) is tested by the irrational world in
which he finds himself. And, although his destiny is not specified at
the end of the drama, Politzer's inference that Karl is to be shipped
across the country on what will prove to be his final journey[43]
illuminates Etienne's own situation and fate.

VI   Los dos verdugos (The Two Executioners)

Arrabal's most autobiographical play, *The Two Executioners*
(1956), places the figure of the mother on stage for the first time.
She denounces her husband to the police and abetted by her older
son Benoit, she seeks to win over her rebellious child, Maurice. At
the same time that she presents herself as a self sacrificing martyr
she exults in her husband's torture and death, even putting salt and
vinegar in his wounds and scratching them. Maurice's steadfast
support of his father and protestations against his mother's actions
finally weaken; at the play's conclusion, Benoit persuades him to
kiss her and to ask for forgiveness.

The identification of the mother with the forces of tyranny in
Spain is communicated visually by the equation of the home with
police headquarters and the torture chamber. Political oppression
is shown to have infiltrated and divided the family; the "two
Spains"[44] of this period are incarnated by the brothers. And the
final pardon that Maurice receives from his mother, who represents
the state, is as strained, repressive, and ultimately grotesque as was
the resolution of Spain's internal strife during the post-Civil War
period.

On the biographical level, Benoit is the counterpart of Arrabal's
own brother, who remained steadfastly loyal to his mother and to
the Franco regime, choosing a military career. And Arrabal is read-
ily identifiable with Maurice. On another level however, the two
brothers may be viewed as representing conflicting forces within

Arrabal himself. Although he repudiated his mother and everything that she stood for, Arrabal found it extremely difficult to overcome the attraction that she exerted upon him. The play's conclusion seems to indicate that the playwright, through his characters, has tried and failed to overcome the nefarious influence his mother had upon him. The title of the play refers, on one level, to the two silent representatives of the state,[45] but the real executioners prove to be the Mother and Benoit who kill the innocence, integrity, and sense of justice in the younger boy.

Arrabal's principal artistic weapon in his pointed attack on the injustice and cruelty rampant in Spanish society is the grotesque. Geneviève Serreau's perceptive observation that *The Two Executioners* may ultimately turn out to be comic because the horror of the piece is so intolerable is consonant with the generally accepted definition of the grotesque as the uneasy union of the horrifying and humorous. The prime example is the mother's sadistic pleasure which attains a level of near orgiastic hysteria when she goes to rub salt and vinegar into the wounds of her suffering husband.[46] The dehumanization often associated with the grotesque mode enters through the visual image of the father bound to a pole by the executioners as if he were a beast of prey killed by hunters. *The Two Executioners* is a prime example of Arrabal's ability to superimpose the political horrors of fascist Spain upon the psychological traumas he himself suffered. The atmosphere helps to communicate the author's theme and, in erasing all vestiges of separation between the worlds of reality and nightmare, anticipates one of the directions Arrabal's later theater will take.

VII   Oraison (Orison)

Orison (1957) utilizes the childlike characters generally associated with Arrabal's earlier works to question the concepts of good and evil. The play is virtually actionless. The setting is a funeral parlor where a couple prays before the coffin of the child they have murdered. Fidio suggests that they change their ways and become good; he uses a Bible to try to define that concept to Lilbé. The dialogue exposes the naiveté of both characters and concludes with a rather tentative affirmation by Fidio that they will attempt to modify their mode of behavior.

In a manner similar to *Fando and Lis, Orison* engages our interest through its presentation of a relationship. Lilbé, like Lis, is the dominant character, despite the fact that Fidio seemingly takes the initiative in deciding that they will be good and in regaling Lilbé with Bible stories. The rhythm of *Orison* derives from Fidio's alternation between exaltation and discouragement as Lilbé's doubts, questions, and use of her sensuality all combine to confuse him and to temper his enthusiasm. The play reflects the absence of any definite moral standard and the bewilderment that Fidio and Lilbé experience illustrates both the suppression of genuine morality in a totalitarian regime and the helplessness of all men in the modern world. The simplicity and repetitiveness of the dialogue mirrors the language of the Bible passages which Fidio reads; the similarity between the two suggests that the Bible is as useless a source of knowledge concerning the true meaning of good and evil as are the libidinous thoughts and actions of Lilbé.

Several essential ingredients in the play which have already become hallmarks of Arrabal's theater are music, ritual and humor. As in *Ceremony for an Assassinated Black,* specific recordings are called for by the author.[47] The title links the play with religious ceremony; the use of music, the nature of the basic set, and dramatic rhythm, with its periodic outbursts of exaltation consistently dissipating into frustration and depression, all combine to lend a ritualistic quality to the work. The perverse nature of the ceremony expresses the playwright's feelings concerning the efficacy of religion and its rituals as a deterrent to evil. Humor results from the clash between the juvenile nature of the characters and their dialogue and the cruelty of Lilbé's thoughts. When she asks whether they will still be able to poke out the eyes of dead people,[48] the audience laughs as a defense against the horror of that idea and as a response to the innocent tone that Lilbé employs in asking the question. And when Fidio tells Lilbé that they must visit someone who is old and poor and paralyzed rather than kill him, she is legitimately confused and comments: "Poor old man" (p. 20). In the cruel, frightening world that produced these characters and that now confronts them, Lilbé's solution has become as logical as Fidio's. The latter's narration of the life of Christ acquires the charm of a *villancico* (Spanish Christmas carol); the lyrical quality it brings to the work clashes with the horror of Christ's passion and man's dilemma. Religion, rather than providing an answer to basic, existential questions, merely functions to underscore the anguish of modern-day man.

VIII   El cementerio de automóviles (The Car Cemetery)⁴⁹

The Car Cemetery (1957) treats many of the same themes as
Orison, but in a richer, more complex, and more highly developed
form. The central question of *Orison,* the nature of good and evil,
is pursued in *The Car Cemetery* as well. And the parody of the
Bible found in the earlier play is echoed in the burlesque treatment
of the passion of Christ. Both works utilize similarly childlike language to narrate the story of Jesus' early years and both introduce a
case of infanticide to depict the slaughter of innocence and purity,
an inevitable consequence of the chaos and immorality of society
and its institutions.

The setting for *The Car Cemetery* is an automobile graveyard, a
microcosm of society, run by Milos and Dila. The services they provide the residents of the establishment include Dila's sexual favors,
"rooms" in the remains of cars, and a urinal for those in need of
one. Emanou and his fellow jazz musicians, Fodère and Topé,
entertain the poor nightly. Emanou is in love with Dila, who warns
him whenever the police are seeking him. Topé betrays him to the
authorities, and Lasca and Tiossido, trainer and athlete respec-
tively, turn into police who flagellate Emanou and crucify him on a
bicycle. As the play concludes, several inhabitants of the graveyard
murder a newborn infant, and Tiossido and Lasca reverse their
original roles and resume their campaign to set a new world record.

As in a number of Arrabal's earlier plays, a trio of male characters reminiscent of the Marx Brothers figures in the action of the
work; in this case, the fact that Fodère is mute links him directly
with Harpo, lending further credence to the nexus between the
cinema and Arrabal's theater. Role reversals involving the master-
slave relationship give structure and meaning to the play; their significance transcends that of the metamorphosis of characters
encountered in previous works. In Hegelian terms, this relationship
reflects the dialectical situation in which the master becomes depen-
dent on the slave through whom he reaches a consciousness of himself; the reversal is then able to take place.⁵⁰

The circular structure derives largely from the movements of
Lasca and Tiossido who begin and conclude the work by seeking a
new record, but in reverse roles. Their relationship reflects both the
indomitable will of the ambitious mother and the male's need to
assert himself physically in response to the feelings of inferiority he
experiences when he compares himself to the female. Lasca and

Tiossido also represent the state and its tyrannical order. At the play's conclusion, the absurdity of their confining, suffocating route is affirmed, and their potential to metamorphose into police serving the system remains unchanged.

Emanou and his morality constitute an integral component of the thematic fiber of the play. His role as a Christ figure is overly explicit; Arrabal seems to be caricaturing both his own parable and the original myth in order to communicate the distortion imposed upon the story of Christ by modern civilization, a distortion that deprives it of all meaning. Like other Arrabalian characters, Emanou lies and murders. But he has memorized the meaning of goodness, so he is convinced that he will be saved: "Well, when we're good, we experience a great inner joy born of peace of spirit that is revealed to us when we see that we resemble the ideal man."[51] Emanou's resemblance to the "ideal man" is all too apparent, but only seems to condemn him in the antiChristian world in which he lives. He plays for the poor because it is impossible to put them out of their misery by killing them all; and he praises Dila for her goodness which he equates with her willingness to accommodate all men sexually. When he does kill, Emanou always makes a point of bringing flowers to the grave of his victim. Such concern for other human beings, which purposely creates tension by also violating traditional moral standards, ultimately emerges as more humane than the society which employs mechanized "automatons" as police who squelch all human feelings. The love shared by Dila and Emanou seems to set off the social mechanism that leads to Emanou's passion and death. If Christ can be thought of as love, then both he and that emotion are abrogated by the mechanized, dehumanized world of the automobile graveyard.

The cemetery becomes a symbol of the wreckage of civilization, of the moral destructiveness of technological society. Visually, the symbol recalls Jean-Luc Godard's use of the automobile in *Weekend;* the staging of the play should engender an immediate apprehension in the audience. The political dimension inheres in the organization of the graveyard. Milos is at once the servant of the residents and the tyrannical despot. When Tiossido implies that he does not have an identity card, Milos instantly becomes threatening and abusive; when the card's substitute (the number on Tiossido's shirt) is produced, Milos reacts to that purposely ludicrous symbol of totalitarian regimentation by reverting to his hypocritically servile demeanor. As José Ortega suggests, *The Car Cemetery* is a play in which Milos incarnates authoritative paternalism, aggression, and the collective neurosis of a people who, under Franco's repressive regime, have lost the ability to overcome the conflict between themselves and the "other."[52] The murder of the infant, the crucifixion of Emanou, and the obsessive and meaningless quest of Tiossido and Lasca all contribute to the play's depiction of the repressive nature of the fascist state in Spain.

The Car Cemetery — with its emphases on the game, on the union of religious ceremony and the grotesque parody of that ceremony, and on the metamorphoses of characters — evinces an enriched artistic vocabulary utilizing earlier motifs, and anticipates the baroque aesthetic of the Panic ceremonies of the 1960s. The play's highly visual nature lends itself to a total theater approach in the Artaudian tradition;[53] this sort of staging will come to characterize the productions of Arrabal's dramas during the following decade. *The Car Cemetery* stands out as one of Arrabal's most ambitious and noteworthy accomplishments of this early period.

IX Les Amours impossibles (The Impossible Loves)[54]

The Impossible Loves (1957) is a short, farcical treatment of the nature of love in which Arrabal interjects an element of grotesque parody by introducing perversion and brutality into the childlike world of the fairy tale. The lovely princess experiences the ecstasy of "pure love" when she meets the haughty dogheaded prince. Love's other dimension, that of pure sensuality, is introduced through the figure of the bullheaded prince. The princess engages in acts of physical love with him, but warns him that her heart belongs to another. When the dogheaded prince returns, the princess is powerless to prevent her jealous, physically aggressive lover from murdering him. Having dispatched his rival, the bullheaded prince expires from the pangs of unrequited love. The distraught princess sees her father approaching and kills herself before he arrives. The father, who has an elephant's head and trunk, addresses his deceased child in the following manner: "Yes, my daughter. I know only too well the meaning of 'impossible loves.' "[55] He then caresses her with his trunk, revealing the incestuous nature of his love as well as its necrophilous component; his passion grows in intensity until the curtain descends.

Love's most painful aspects are evoked in this mysterious, poetic, and grotesque piece. Death is accompanied by rhythmic barks and belches which dehumanize and mock man's suffering and destruction, an attempt to combat the fear and anguish produced by the senselessness of the life cycle. The two aspects of love are completely separated throughout the work; their division produces man's frustrations which can only be reconciled in death. The figure of the father combines those two components of love into a unified expression of human feeling (albeit incestuous). The two facets of love depicted in the play also suggest the division into the two Spains and allude indirectly to the various contradictory elements in Arrabal himself, notably the dualistic nature of his feelings toward his country, his mother, and himself. The father's frenetic expression of a suppressed, unacceptable passion combines the horror and shock of necrophilia and incest with the tenderness of spiritual love. The play's final image, then, focuses on the father's anguish and constitutes a moving and disturbing evocation of the dialectical nature of love and of life and its effect on man.

X   Concert dans un oeuf (Concert in an Egg)

Concert in an Egg (1948) is Arrabal's first play directly inspired by a specific work of art (Hieronymous Bosch's painting of the same title). The play harkens back to themes of previous works but also foreshadows Panic works and performances of the 1960s.

Concert in an Egg is divided into two perfectly symmetrical acts of seven scenes each. The odd numbered scenes advance the "plot," tracing the course of the relationship between Filtos and Li. The even numbered scenes present in mime the relationship between two couples of different generations. Virtually every scene concludes with the projection of slides for a specified amount of time, with music in the background. The action is limited to a series of vignettes in counterpoint which trace Li's influence upon the quixotic Filtos and portray the latter's unsuccessful attempt to secure her love. Filtos departs on his motorcycle to continue his mission, and the perverse inhabitants of the world responsible for his failure mock him, dismissing both him and his quest as insane.

Concert in an Egg contains ten characters, the exact number of musicians depicted in Bosch's painting. The aura of evil that surrounds the Flemish townsmen in the eggshell is reflected in the character of many of the people in the play. The idea of metamorphosis suggested by one figure in the painting whose head is becoming a castle is communicated both by the action of the play and by the use of slides of other paintings by Bosch and by Pieter Breugel. The latter's work, The *Tower of Babel,* is shown repeatedly after the even numbered scenes; it reiterates the motif of the castle while also reinforcing the idea of human egocentricity and lack of communication expressed in the mimed action. The musical motif suggested by the title is implemented through symmetrical, precise repetitions both within and between the two acts. The result is a form of counterpoint, a literary fugue based on the themes of love and goodness in contrast with hypocrisy and repression. The conclusion, the intermittent use of loud rock and roll music following silent scenes, and the thematic linking of odd and even numbered scenes through the use of precisely timed slide presentations all combine to produce a carefully controlled musical cacophony which underscores the artist's attempt to impose order on the irrational world.

Here, as in *The Car Cemetery,* Arrabal utilizes a myth to expose the degeneracy of society. *Concert in an Egg* is subtitled "Quixotic Ceremony"; various references throughout the play link Filtos with Don Quixote. Arrabal's praise of Franz Kafka's observation that Sancho Panza is really a demon who tempts the idealistic Don[56] may have inspired structuring the work around the relationship between Li, a surrogate Sancho, and Filtos. The latter renounces his vow of chastity when he meets Li, but ultimately fails to realize his desire for a complete love and is rejected by Li in favor of the Man. All aspects of love are presented in the play. The repressive forces of society that pervert genuine love are identified as the family (Act I, scenes 4 and 6; Act 2, scene 2); societal institutions (war — Act 2, scene 4); and false morality (the older generation of voyeurs — Act 2, scene 6). Even an innocuous action, setting the dinner table, is shown to contain perversity (Act 2, scene 4). The two young girls who appear in the scenes with Li and Filtos are prime examples of hypocrisy; their childish games and laughter cloak their disdain for all human feeling.

Concert in an Egg contains allusions to other plays by Arrabal; Filtos appears to be an older Fando whose memory of Lis and her death has never been eradicated. The role reversals involving Li and the Man resemble those in *The Car Cemetery;* and the use of a myth to demonstrate the world's rejection of an ideal (Christ, Don Quixote) also points to that work. Filtos' search for goodness and reference to the purity of the angels suggests *Orison,* as he himself states. *Concert in an Egg* is, in part, an attempt to assess previous efforts directed toward finding goodness and logic in a perverse world. By setting the play on the beach, Arrabal evokes the memory of his father,[57] acknowledging the role that his absent parent must play in his personal quest for psychic wholeness. The circularity of structure both looks backward and projects the author-protagonist into the future, suggesting an ongoing cycle in which Filtos (inspired by his father's memory and by the love he experienced, albeit momentarily, in the boat) will continue his search.

Gloria Orenstein's discussion of the symbol of the egg in Leonora Carrington's theater helps to elucidate its significance in *Concert in an Egg*. She comments that "many of her works relate the alchemical symbol of the egg (the alchemist's oven in which black primal matter is transformed into gold) to the female symbol of the egg, suggesting that it is through woman that the spiritual transformation of humanity will occur."[58] Filtos' search for the perfect woman is essentially a quest for spiritual harmony for himself and for all men. He is not immune to the corruptive elements of life, but his alienation from the world, although painful for him, is largely encouraging.

The insidious nature of the world against which Filtos struggles is conveyed by the clash between the perfect order of the drama's structure and the chaos and disharmony encapsulated within that order. In a sense, *Concert in an Egg* is a parody of the classical world; the perverse girls who comment on Filtos' actions and ultimate failure constitute a grotesque caricature of the Greek chorus. The Baroque world of Miguel de Cervantes' *Don Quixote* is made "classical" to underscore, by contrast, the even greater violence and irrationality of contemporary existence. Filtos' symmetrical arrival and departure leaves the dream-like world of Arrabal's theater largely unchanged, but *he* is not the same. By gently tucking in the Man and Li before leaving, Filtos confirms his transcendence of life's perverseness; his "failure" does not constitute defeat, but rather spiritual renewal.

XI Guérnica[59]

Arrabal's first play to be set in a specific time and place, *Guérnica* (1959) unites a timeless Spanish myth[60] with the childlike characters, dream-like ambience, and dark humor that have come to characterize his theater. The play's protagonists, Fanchou and Lira, are in many ways an elderly Fando and Lis.[61] Their mutual alienation is communicated by their physical separation. A note of black humor is interjected into the piece by having Lira trapped in the toilet as a result of the air raid.

The play's structure is based on a number of repetitive occurrences. Each successive bombing leaves Lira more completely trapped under stones, until she is totally submerged. The most concrete evocation of the Picasso painting (the inspiration for the work), the periodic crossing of the stage by a woman and her child, also points toward the conclusion; the mother's final appearance is with a coffin which has replaced the child. The intermittent entrances of the officer, the writer, and the journalist also link the themes of the work with its structure. A final air raid destroys Fanchou and Lira, but their spirits survive in the form of two balloons that float upward, escaping successfully the rifle fire of the enraged and frustrated officer.

The highly visual nature of the play is due in part to the inspiration Arrabal found in Picasso's masterpiece. The subtitle of the Spanish version of the play, "The Disasters of War," suggests a desire to emulate the black humor, visual impact and socio-political protest found in Francisco Goya as well. *Guérnica* refers to a specific atrocity in a fixed time and place, but Arrabal's characterizations, his evocation of a traditional myth, the influences of other artists, and the horrors of other wars all contribute universality. Fanchou and Lira are at once innocent victims of the Spanish Civil War and of all wars and representatives of the human weakness and insensitivity leading to destructive quarrels. As John Kronik has commented: "To the extent that they function metaphorically in the play as a microcosm of human relationships, they illustrate the lesson that man has a warring nature, that he cannot coexist, even in the most ideal relationship, without conflict."[62] Their egocentric bickering, suggestive at once of puerility and of senility, may represent the two Spains in conflict; but it also has a broader meaning. Fanchou's reluctance to exert himself to extricate Lira, his rebukes directed at her ignorance of the nature of war, Lira's references to Fanchou's sexual impotence and her utilization of the "silent treatment" are both humorous and disquieting in the context of the desperate situation.

Minor characters in *Guérnica* contribute to both the visual and the thematic impact of the drama. The mother and child, who transport arms across the stage six times until the child is killed, link the play with the Picasso painting, underscoring the theme of the destruction of innocence. Yet at the same time their "mission" reinforces the antiheroic nature of the play, evoking, to an extent, the vision of war found in Bertold Brecht's *Mother Courage.*[63] The officer devouring a sandwich on stage is reminiscent of the Judge in *The Labyrinth;* both typify the unfeeling, repressive nature of society's institutions and their representatives. The writer who shows no concern for the plight of Fanchou and Lira, thinking of them only as material he can utilize, epitomizes human greed and hypocrisy. The vacuous, cliché ridden phrases he utters in communicating the "true spirit" of the conflict in Spain represent Arrabal's attack on both the Spanish tradition of rhetoric and the limitations of a purely verbal theater.[64] The writer is a symbol for those men who came to bleed Spain for inspiration while watching her choke on her own lifeblood. He is the last character to speak in the play; his ecstatic delight at the thought of the novel he will create out of death and destruction confirms the decadence of his form of art.

Although the final words are spoken by the writer, they do not determine the character and impact of the work's conclusion. Before he speaks, two balloons representing the spirit of Lira and Fanchou float majestically skyward despite the officer's attempt to shoot them down. After the sound of the writer's voice has faded away, the noise of soldiers marching is heard, gradually drowned by a chorus of voices singing "Guernikako arbola." Throughout the play, Lira, despite her predicament, asks Fanchou to see if the famous tree of Guérnica is still standing. The chorus rejoicing at the miracle of the tree's escape sounds a note of hope for freedom which to a degree mitigates the horrors of war and the pettiness of the elderly couple's quarrels. Arrabal himself has declared that the play's conclusion is decidedly optimistic.[65] *Guérnica* portrays the destruction by war of the innocent, yet also affirms the indestructibility of the human spirit. Man's myths (Don Quixote, Christ, and now the tree of Guérnica) have been presented in conflict with the perverse nature of the world; as long as these myths survive, man's aspirations will have a focus and source of inspiration assuring the continuance of hope.[66]

XII   La Bicyclette du condamné (The Condemned Man's Bicycle)

The final play published by Arrabal before his three year respite from dramatic production, *The Condemned Man's Bicycle*[67] has always produced a strong emotional effect upon its author because of his intense empathy with the protagonist, Viloro.[68] The latter struggles throughout to play a simple C major scale successfully on the piano. He is encouraged by his girl friend, Tasla, but mocked by two mysterious male characters. Tasla's job consists of transporting condemned prisoners in a cage attached to her bicycle. The prisoner Paso appears alternately in the cage and then inexplicably free. While at liberty, he joins the two men in deriding Viloro's efforts at the piano. Periodically, this trio places increasingly greater constraints upon Viloro's physical movements, warning that worse will follow if he does not desist from playing. Paradoxically, his musical success increases in direct proportion to the restraints imposed upon him.

The climax occurs when Viloro is murdered by Paso and his cohorts while playing his scale impeccably. A chastened Tasla comes for him (she had engaged in lewd acts with the two men earlier), transporting a coffin with the bicycle instead of a cage. She gently places him inside and departs. Offstage, children's mocking laughter is heard, muffled by the sound of perfect scales, played progressively louder as the curtain descends.

The cyclical nature of *The Condemned Man's Bicycle* (as underscored by the structure of the work, the metamorphosis of the characters and their situations, the repetitive exchange of the same gifts by Viloro and Tasla, and the patterns of the musical notes themselves) reflects with mathematical precision the chaos and confusion of life.[69] The idea of the circle as dramatic structure is again suggested by the visual symbol of the bicycle and is reinforced here by a blue ball (the gift exchanged by Viloro and Tasla a number of times which floats skyward at the play's conclusion). The cyclical alternations of a free Paso and a confined Viloro and vice-versa give impetus to the linear action of the play, moving toward the annihilation of Viloro while contributing to the central conceit of the confining, labyrinthine nature of life. The confusion concerning the true identity of the condemned man links Viloro and Paso, implying that their relationship is of major significance in the identification of the play's principal themes.

Viloro is the only character whose essential nature does not undergo a metamorphosis. He thus becomes the central figure in an obsessive nightmare which ultimately engulfs him. That nightmare, while reflecting the repressive nature of external reality, also appears to be of his own making. Paso is a sort of alter ego, an assertive, libidinous character who can reject feminine advances or instigate his own sexual conquests at will. Raymond-Mundschau suggests that Paso represents what Viloro would like to be and cannot;[70] Viloro's fear of the external world seems to contain elements of psychological tyrannization projected on reality. Viloro's struggle with himself should not be viewed as self-defeating, however. At the play's conclusion, Tasla kicks Paso in the head and then tenderly lifts Viloro into the coffin.

Viloro's struggle with himself and the world is communicated primarily through his attempt to master the musical scale, an attempt which meets with success only when he is forced to deal with society's oppressions. This situation communicates Arrabal's own view of the artist's source of inspiration, suggesting that literature or art can be truly meaningful only when it considers sociological questions as well as aesthetic or philosophic ones. Tasla's lascivious acts with the silent characters representative of repressive forces in society are symptomatic of life's mutability and deceit. Viloro's struggle to reconcile opposing forces through the union of love and pain is evident in Tasla's request to "send me a kiss for every stroke of the whip they give the condemned man."[71] Here as before, Arrabal seeks the resolution through art of the dialectical forces which confuse and restrain man's noblest pursuits; he is only able to find it, however, in death.

The Condemned Man's Bicycle manages to be an optimistic work despite the destruction of the author-artist; it examines the theme of freedom and condemnation within the context of the artist-society relationship. As Messerman states: "Paradoxically, then, artistic freedom or creation for Arrabal grew out of repression. The derisive laughter of the *bourreaux* may also be seen as that of his family who mocked his early attempts to write, or as that of society who would deny the artist any freedom of experimentation."[72] But as the play's conclusion indicates, internal (family) and external (society — censorship) restraints have not silenced the author. Viloro, the childish, creative component of man's spirit, triumphs over Paso, the stronger, more physical element. The music is not silenced; Viloro is killed, but his art transcends his physical being and remains vital. The blue ball, symbolic of the childlike world of Arrabal's artistic endeavors, rises above all attempts at repression, affirming the accomplishments of the young author. *The Condemned Man's Bicycle,* then, constitutes a dramatic affirmation of the efficacy of art as a socio-psychological expression of man's hopes, fears, and aspirations.

In analyzing the theater of Arrabal's first period, Bernard Gille identifies two principal visions: an inner-directed, subjective presentation of the author's psychologically imprisoning childhood and a more mature, open ended focus upon the future liberation of man through thought, language and games.[73] Any schema that seeks to take a rich and diverse body of literary works and fit them into restrictive categories can achieve only a limited success. Nevertheless, Gille's analysis does contribute to an overview of the plays written before 1960. The inclusion of a third vision — that of man trapped by irrational and repressive socio-political forces — would provide a more complete schema accommodating the diverse themes and artistic techniques utilized by the playwright.

As has been noted, a dominant feature of Arrabal's early theater is the childlike nature of many of his characters. Their central roles interject a lyrical note, adding pathos and dramatic impact as a result of their vain struggle to reconcile self-image with accepted social norms. Fidio and Lilbé, Emanou and Filtos all seek insight into the nature of goodness; but within the context of their dramatic milieu (reflecting the reality of Spain's totalitarian government), that concept is shown to be devoid of real meaning.

Despite their obvious physical superiority, the male characters in many early plays emerge as naive and insecure in comparison with their female counterparts. Lis dominates Fando, Lilbé's cynicism tempers Fidio's naive optimism, and Dila and Lira use their sexuality to control their relationships with Emanou and Fanchu. The tensions and conflicts of these relationships add psychological depth; Arrabal utilizes these tensions on one level to examine and seek resolution of his own psychic concerns. The character traits of these personages lend credence to Gille's observation that a dominant vision in Arrabal's early theater is that of imprisoning puerility. The influence of the mother figure, identified with the state and its repression, adds political and psychological impact to the dilemma; this is evidenced by such characters as Fando, unable to realize a mature love, and Maurice, who succumbs to the stultifying influence of the Jungian "devouring mother" while still a child. Likewise, Fidio and Lilbé, all of the principal characters in *The Tricycle,* and the two vagabonds in *Ceremony for an Assassinated Black* fail to reconcile their childish instincts with the oppressive

morality of the genuinely immoral modern world. A major component of Arrabal's early theater is his view of man in a pure, natural
state, bewildered, oppressed, and psychologically traumatized by
diverse socio-political forces infiltrating his inner dream world (the
subconscious) and impinging upon his thoughts and actions.

Other early plays rely less on the creation of a highly subjective,
juvenile ambience than on an externalization of identifiable, societal institutions. Both types of plays share a dream-like quality that
permeates the setting and tone of the work. But the nightmarish
ambience of *The Labyrinth* and the mythic dimensions of *Guérnica*
(the tree), *The Car Cemetery* (Christ), and *Concert in an Egg* (Don
Quixote) are far removed from the purely subjective vision of a
playwright expressing highly personal, psychological concerns.
Arrabal presents and examines the human condition through his
focus upon our labyrinthine, kafkaesque existence. The true
exploitative nature of war, first considered in *Picnic on the Battlefield,* receives a fuller treatment in *Guérnica,* a play at once more
specific and more universal in nature. The exploration of the relationship between the Arrabalian Christ and Don Quixote and the
dramatic world they must confront provides insights into human
existence transcending subjective preoccupations and personal concerns. Arrabal's early theater constitutes a search for liberation on
the part of the author, and ultimately on behalf of all mankind. As
Gille has suggested, language and games are at once components of
that search and the tools to be used in achieving its goal. The metamorphoses of characters, the cyclical patterns in the plays, the use
of balloons, balls and bicycles, and the delight in nonsense dialogue
and absurd games of logic all combine to illustrate both the confining nature of the universe and the weapons that can be utilized to
surmount its constraints.

As a young writer struggling with his personal psychological
traumas and with his nascent career, Arrabal expressed self doubts,
insecurities and pessimism in these plays. Yet even in these first
endeavors there was a note of hope, the affirmation of an ongoing
struggle, as seen in the tricycle which moves again, in Filtos continuance of his quest, and in Vincent and Jerome's staging of a
play. As marriage and artistic recognition came to Arrabal, they
were accompanied by a greater feeling of liberation and sense of
unlimited possibilities. If Arrabal, identifying with Viloro, envied
the physical aggressiveness and self assurance of Paso, he nevertheless affirmed himself and his own artistic spirit in the conclusion of

The Condemned Man's Bicycle. Growth in self assurance as an artist and man was a necessary prelude to the foundation of his own, unique literary movement. So too were the experiments with the chaotic milieu of *The Labyrinth,* the complex structure and multiple character metamorphoses of *The Car Cemetery,* the mathematical precision of structure of *Concert in an Egg* and *The Condemned Man's Bicycle,* and the concept of theater as ceremony, exemplified by *Orison* and *Ceremony for an Assassinated Black.* All of these were to find expression in Arrabal's Panic Movement. And some early plays would receive Panic productions by the Argentine directors who became Arrabal's collaborators during the 1960s. Arrabal's three year respite (1959–1962) from the writing of plays constituted a period of personal and artistic growth. When he resumed his dramatic production, it was with renewed energy and inspiration. Some basic characteristics of his Panic theater had already been established, but a significant expansion in artistic technique and objectives was soon to take place.

CHAPTER 3

"Panic" Theater

T HE ideology of the Panic Movement was already reflected to a significant degree in Arrabal's theater of the 1950s. The first formal meeting of the creators of "Panique" — Arrabal, Alejandro Jodorowsky, and Roland Topor — at the Café de la Paix in Paris did not occur, however, until 1960. The initial term adopted to describe their view of the world and of art was "burlesque" (an expression which purposely evoked both the style of the Baroque Spanish poet, Góngora, and the ambience of the American strip tease). The word "Panique" was originated in September, 1962;[1] shortly thereafter Arrabal published *Cinq récits paniques (Five Panic Narratives)* in the Surrealist journal, *La Brèche,* edited by André Breton. Lectures, expositions, and theatrical events followed in rapid succession, and the number of participating artists increased substantially. The success of the venture was highlighted by the following: the National Theater of London's production of Arrabal's *L'Architecte et l'Empereur d'Assyrie (The Architect and the Emperor of Assyria)* in 1967, the regular appearance of Topor's drawings in the *New York Times,* and the release of Jodorowsky's film *El topo,* the final work presented at the Cannes Film Festival of 1971, which subsequently enjoyed tremendous popularity in the United States.

Although Arrabal has stated that he has no theory of the theater, that writing is an adventure for him and does not constitute the fruit of knowledge or experience,[2] his exposition of the concepts of Panic can provide insight into his methodology of theater. His most complete presentation of the theoretical basis of Panic is contained in the lecture delivered on the subject at Sydney University, Australia, August, 1963.[3] The short essay entitled "Theater as 'Panic' Ceremony," written in 1966, explicates tenets and methods of Panic. Some indication has already been given of the extent to

58

which earlier plays anticipate the theories and techniques of the movement. A consideration of those theories should shed further light on the dramas already discussed and make the forthcoming analysis of Arrabal's plays of the 1960s more efficacious.

I *"Panic" Man and "Panic" Theater*

"Panic" for Arrabal is neither an artistic group or literary movement, but a lifestyle governed by confusion, humor, terror, chance, and euphoria.[4] In stating that he does not really know exactly what "Panic" is, that it is more of an antimovement than a movement, Arrabal interjects a note of dialectical tension into his theorizing which parallels its counterpart in his literary endeavors. Panic is at once a serious exposition of philosophical and aesthetic principles and a parody of attempts at organized literary movements and theories.[5] This quality is suggested by the Greek god Pan, the source of the name "Panic." Pan, which means "everything," was a buffoon in his childhood, and then later became the terrifying figure — half goat, half man — who frightened people by leaping out in front of them unexpectedly. Both the name and its etymology suited Arrabal's purposes perfectly, communicating the confusion and instability of his theatrical world through their allusion to a duality of form (man-goat) and aesthetic technique (humor-fear). As Arrabal has stated, his Panic theater "neither modern, nor avant-garde, nor new, nor absurd, aspires only to be infinitely free and better."[6]

The key principles providing the philosophical basis for "Panic" are chance and memory. Arrabal begins his exposition of the ideology of the Panic Movement with the following truism: the past was once the future. The future "acts" in what he terms "coups de théâtre," in response to confusion or chance. He rejects attempts at perfection as sterile and inhuman; all that is truly human must reflect the confusion of life. By a mock-serious process of mathematical calculations and formulae, Arrabal concludes that life is memory and man is chance.[7] Having established the essential nature of life, Arrabal then seeks to define the role of the artist in light of his precepts. He concludes that "the more the work of the artist is governed by chance, confusion and the unexpected, the more it will be rich, stimulating and fascinating" (p. 48).

The primary aesthetic of Panic theater is based on the union of opposites. The Panic writer converts his dramas into parties or ceremonies combining tragedy and *guignol,* poetry and vulgarity, comedy and melodrama, love and eroticism, the "happening" and mathematical set theory, bad taste and aesthetic refinement, sacrilege and the sacred, putting to death and the exaltation of life, the sordid and the sublime.[8] Arrabal's enumeration of the characteristics of the Panic Man and his work includes many qualities found in his own theater. Among the themes identified as suitable are the author himself, sex, humor, reality (up to and including the nightmare), the sordid and, of course, memory, chance and confusion. The author's integral role in his work has already been demonstrated; the union of reality and nightmare encountered in several pre-1960 plays, including *The Two Executioners* and *The Labyrinth,* intensifies in the following decade.

Considering the Panic Man's artistic endeavors, Arrabal rejects suspense and irony and affirms the epic, ambiguity and non-ambiguity, mathematics and systematization — and contradiction. The precision with which his works are constructed and the use of the grotesque (the union of the horrifying and the comic) and of metamorphoses and cycles underscore the importance he attaches to confusion and contradiction as aesthetic devices supporting his view of life and uniting theme and form in his dramas. This pervasive dialectical tension is reinforced in Arrabal's enumeration of "phantasms" of the Panic Man. In addition to paranoia, despair, jealousy, fetishes, necrophilia, mythology and mythomania, these include an antithetical pair: megalomania and modesty.

"Panic," then, is a mock-serious exploration and appraisal of the artist's previous achievements as well as a projection into the future[9] which suggests in abstract and purposely enigmatic terms what subsequent endeavors may be like. Arrabal's exposition of the principles of "Panic" constitutes a tacit announcement of further artistic experiment, undertaken with renewed energy, freedom and increased confidence. During the 1960s the tenets of the Panic Movement serve as a point of departure for Arrabal; additional sources of inspiration and innovation include the Surrealists and their interest in alchemy, the theories of Artaud and Grotowski, and the perspective of the avant-garde Argentine directors (Lavelli, García and Savary). A consideration of these diverse stimuli which mold Arrabal's evolving concept of theater should prove helpful in analyzing his dramas of the 1960's and in explaining his development and success as a playwright.

II   La Communion solennelle (Solemn Communion)

Published in 1963 in the Surrealist journal, *La Brèche, Solemn Communion* is Arrabal's first play written under the Panic banner. A short piece, it suppresses the separation between dream and reality while presenting a highly ritualized vision of a little girl's first communion. The work begins with two men placing a nude, deceased woman into a coffin. Their prayers are interrupted by the appearance of a necrophiliac. They hastily depart with the coffin, pursued by the sexual deviate. The trio of males and the coffin reappear periodically throughout the play; the necrophiliac's state of sexual arousal is progressively heightened with each appearance (as evidenced by the increased length of the snake-like appendage affixed to him). The action of the work is also structured in time by the child's grandmother who dresses the girl in highly baroque vestments while lecturing the communicant incessantly about the virtues of a clean home and the obligations of a dutiful wife, brushing aside the girl's queries about the necrophiliac. After the child has been completely dressed, she and her grandmother start to leave the stage. Their exit is interrupted by the return of the necrophiliac, who, encountering an unguarded coffin, takes advantage of the situation, undressing, handing his clothes to the grandmother, and entering the coffin to make love to the cadaver inside. The child, who had left the stage with her grandmother, returns to observe what is occurring. She then takes out a long knife and plunges it repeatedly into the necrophiliac. As the drama concludes, she laughs hysterically, her dress becomes spattered with blood, and several red balloons float up from inside the coffin.

On one level, the play is a denunciation of the repressive influence of the grandmother, whose traditional views emerge as more perverse and hypocritical than the desires and actions of the necrophiliac.[10] Her seeming lack of interest in the necrophiliac's activities may well be a form of sublimation; the extreme banality of her dialogue introduces a note of humor but also demands that the actress playing the role infuse her words with an energy (probably sexual) belied by their content if the play is to have the desired dramatic impact. The union of religion and sexuality, a feature of Surrealist theater,[11] helps effect a shock at once overt and subliminal in nature. The little girl's violent act is both an expression of sexual florescence (the blood on her dress) and of perverted moral-. ity engendered by the nefarious influence of the grandmother. The red balloons produce multiple responses in the audience and lend themselves to diverse interpretations. They add a touch of incongruous humor by converting drops of blood into something playful, while their shape, as noted in earlier plays by Arrabal, confirms the cyclical, repetitive nature of the Spanish upbringing which inculcates traditional values in generation after generation.

Although the play should not be interpreted (or staged) as a work of the Absurd, some of Martin Esslin's observations about this type of drama do provide insight into *Solemn Communion*. He states: "The Theater of the Absurd, however grotesque, frivolous, and irreverent it may appear, represents a return to the original, religious function of the theater — the confrontation of man with the spheres of myth and religious reality."[12] *Solemn Communion,* as its title suggests, epitomizes theater as ritual. The rite of transubstantiation is integrally linked to eroticism; the girl's union with the flesh of Christ merges with her sexual initiation in a highly stylized fashion, affirming the presence of sensuality in religious ritual and of ritualism in sexuality.

Gloria Orenstein's incisive study of contemporary Surrealist theater provides a philosophical basis for analysis of another dimension of *Solemn Communion.* She considers implications of the elimination of historical or chronological time, a technique that André Breton had foreseen. As she states: "When time reversal is accomplished and simultaneity takes over, the past and the future can merge and create a new present, where the old antinomies are overthrown."[13] She concludes: "With the elimination of all time boundaries and the compression of all space and time into a composite present, the metamorphoses of a being that occur in this continuum permit that being to exist on various levels simultaneously... This multidimensional personality creates the possibility of the intermingling of identities."[14] The total elimination of a feeling of "waking reality" in *Solemn Communion* supports an interpretation of the play based on the absence of chronological time beyond the simple physical act of dressing the young girl. The grandmother and child may then be viewed as one and the same person. The former's lifelong frustrations cause her to examine her own past and to relive the brainwashing she had experienced. The little girl's queries about sex and her final act of violent eroticism occur in the subconscious of the grandmother, where her own repressed desires are harbored. The indifference she has always had to feign toward sensuality is externalized in the memory of her own first communion; but this time the subconscious, libidinous forces suppressed within her emerge in the form of the necrophiliac. Her final action, then, is essentially cathartic; the balloons, while confirming the repetitive nature of psychological indoctrination, also interject a note of rebellion and a definite feeling of emancipation.

Liberation from the constraints of chronological time and from the psychological barriers produced by repressive forces is echoed in visual components of the play. It will become increasingly necessary to consider Arrabal's plays as works for the theater, rather than as pieces of dramatic literature. *Solemn Communion* incorporates visual elements which support the themes of the work, but are also of interest in their own right. The stage directions call for costumes highly baroque in nature. While the use of music is not explicitly called for, Arrabal could not conceive of a production of the piece that did not include substantial aural stimulation.[15] The dominant role of ritual supports the themes of the play, accentuating its impact through the use of stylized movement and action. The periodic transits of the coffin followed by the necrophiliac allow theater space to impress itself on the spectator through the mind's eye. The obsessive nature of the action, the stylizations and baroque excesses contribute a sense of the surreal; actions appear larger than life and the characters acquire mythic dimensions through the invocation of archetypes. *Solemn Communion* was a favorite of André Breton's because it converted his Surrealist vision into a dramatic reality at once frightening, dazzling and disturbing. And by basing that vision on memory and confusion, Arrabal illustrated the efficacy of a theater derived from the principles of Panic.

III   Le Grand Cérémonial (The Grand Ceremonial)

The Grand Ceremonial (1963) continues the analysis of the mother-son relationship begun in *The Two Executioners,* exploring psychological forces affecting the protagonist to a much fuller extent. This long, two-act drama whose two realms merge into a unified oneiric vision, transcends the duality of reality and nightmare in the earlier play. The prologue introduces several motifs which recur repeatedly, reinforcing the obsessive patterns characteristic of a dream. Police sirens (an externalization of Cavanosa's guilt feelings) and the latter's cry of "Mummy, mummy"[16] are heard before the lights come up. Cavanosa, a deformed cripple, meets Sil. She, despite his hostility, falls in love with him, agrees to become his slave and accept the abuse he inflicts upon her, while rejecting her former lover with his traditional manner and conventional handsomeness.

The first act also introduces the protagonist's mother, essentially the same self martyring, guilt provoking, sensuous woman encountered in *The Two Executioners*. She reminds him of the sacrifices she has made for him, alternating between tender sentimentality and cruel displays of sadism. She seems to possess an intuitive understanding and knowledge of all of Cavanosa's thoughts and deeds. After confronting him with his relationship with Sil, his mother leaves him alone with the girl. Cavanosa's ritualistic, dehumanizing actions seem to intesify Sil's sexual desires; the scene culminates in an orgiastic expression of passion in which Sil urges Cavanosa on with growing ecstasy as he proceeds to choke her to death.

The second act begins with the arrival of Sil's former lover. She revives miraculously, joining Cavanosa in rejecting the intruder who comes from the world of normalcy. The mother exerts her own influence, inducing Cavanosa to reject Sil and to return to his "mummy." Sil allows her ex-lover to depart, accepting the conditions upon which her acceptance by Cavanosa and his mother is contingent: she will never see Cavanosa again and will serve as the mother's slave, to be tortured and abused according to her mistress' whim. The two brief final scenes introduce another girl, Lys. Unlike Sil, she suffers from physical and emotional wounds similar to those of Cavanosa. She is unperturbed by his outbursts of anger, his threats and expressions of rejection; he is extremely attractive to her. Her sincerity and naiveté seem to penetrate Cavanosa's insecurities and defense mechanisms; and as the play concludes she induces him to put her into a pram and go off with her. The mother is left behind, muttering, "I'm so unhappy" (p. 215). Whether Lys will become another victim of Cavanosa's perverted sexuality is left uncertain, but the tone of the conclusion is decidedly lyrical, tender, and hopeful.

The Grand Ceremonial is primarily a psychological play; it clearly contains a strong autobiographical component. Arrabal's penchant for self deprecation receives direct expression in the work. His identification with Cavanosa is quite clear; the character's feelings about his mother and his view of himself as deformed recall Arrabal's own feelings expressed in the interview with Alain Schifres. Specific motifs in the play, including Cavanosa's allusion to the small size of his sex organ and need to remain a virgin, echo statements made by Arrabal to Ann Morrisett in the "theatrical" interview published in the *Evergreen Review* several years before this play was written.[17] The name of the protagonist, an anagram of the great lover, Casanova, accentuates the strong note of grotesque deformation. Despite these parodical elements and such Grand Guignolesque scenes as Cavanosa's attempted murder of his mother, when she reacts to the supposed instrument of her death by commenting: "That's what I was afraid of. A knife.... Five hours to die! And this is how you treat your own mother!" (p. 150), the play also manages to capture the intense anguish of its protagonist.

Cavanosa is essentially an adolescent Fando (the link between the two plays is reinforced by allusions in *The Grand Ceremonial* to a pram and a chain [p. 130] and to the fact that Sil is not paralyzed [p. 167]). Cavanosa suffers from a complex caused by a fixation on the mother figure which does not allow him to integrate his two parents in his psyche or develop an independent personality and ego.[18] On the psychological level the play portrays Cavanosa's struggle to overcome the influence of the mother; the police sirens reflect the duality of his feelings toward her (the need to "kill" her and guilt from his growing consciousness of that need). To free himself from both his feelings and their origin, Cavanosa seeks liberation through a woman. His mother struggles to counter his efforts, utilizing her seductive charms and encouraging Cavanosa to express his feelings and frustrations with life-sized dolls. Sil, the dolls, and the mother all come to represent the pernicious element of sexuality that culminates in destruction. (The mother gave Cavanosa his first doll as a gift; he picks small coffins as presents for her, for his favorite doll, and also for Sil.)

The sacrifice of Sil, essentially another nonvital doll, is presented as the continuance of a nightly ritual, more fantasy than reality. Within the context of the dream-like atmosphere, it becomes an affirmation of Cavanosa's ongoing neurosis which precludes psychic escape and positive action. Cavanosa's reprehensible treatment of Sil is really a reaction to his growing fear of realizing his repressed desires.[19] Death, violence, and eroticism intermingle; the mother's incestuous longing for her own son takes the form of a wish to die by his hand and helps to explain the warped nature of Cavanosa's own feelings of love, evidenced by his treatment of his dolls and Sil. Physical torture becomes an expression of internal strife, and physical deformity the externalization of psychic anguish. While these forces dominate, the play's atmosphere remains subsumed by the world of the subconscious.

The only "realistic" scenes of the play are those between Lys and Cavanosa. As a representative of the pure component of femininity, Lys emerges as Sil's alterego (affirmed by their names which are palindromes one of the other); she finds Cavanosa lovable and attractive because she has not had contact with other men. Like Cavanosa, Lys is a product of repression (Spain); her ingenuousness and empathy penetrate Cavanosa's defenses in a manner that Sil's pity never could. Arrabal refers to Cavanosa's decision to take her with him in the carriage and leave his mother behind as the most beautiful happy ending in all of his theater.[20] Cavanosa says to Lys at the play's conclusion: "Let's go. Your eyes burn to look into my eyes, your hands are aflame to hold mine, your back is lily-white for me to scourge, your voice is full of sorrow for your death" (p. 215). If his words introduce a note of ambiguity by suggesting that love is still only possible as a destructive act ending in death, his tender kissing of Lys and the fact that he speaks "dreamily" to her justify, at least partially, the feeling of hope for the protagonist's liberation from the imprisoning influence of the archetypal devouring mother.

The Grand Ceremonial demonstrates a significant advance over The Two Executioners both in the psychological development of its author-protagonist and its dramatic technique. The two plays are linked by the figure of the mother and by several specific motifs, most notably the mother's wish to pour salt and vinegar into the wound of the male she dominates. In The Grand Ceremonial, Cavanosa's wound is produced by his mother's kiss; love and pain, eroticism and destruction thereby all fuse. Cavanosa speaks of expressing love by whipping a girl until her back is one large gaping wound; and the mother says passionately to her son: "Hurt me, scratch me, widen this gaping wound in my heart — pitilessly" (p. 139). The image is central to the play's vision of love; although that vision persists at the play's conclusion, it is tempered by tenderness. Through Lys, Cavanosa may finally reconcile the violent component of love with its gentler aspects.

The Grand Ceremonial, Arrabal's most penetrating psychological play, is less a Panic work than some earlier dramas and many subsequent ones. Its coherent vision of a tortured psyche does not emphasize confusion and chance and it suppresses the tendency toward metamorphosis of character. Yet, on the aesthetic level, it does demand, as its title indicates, a staging utilizing ritual in a manner transcending psychological concerns. The lover may be viewed as representing the bourgeois world; he is cold, mannered and artificial. As a theatrical character, he suggests an antivital, conventional drama. The aesthetic of deformation and the grotesque, crystallized by Ramón del Valle-Inclán, would be incarnated by Cavanosa. This theater is based on pain, insecurity, ugliness, eroticism and anguish — in other words: life. The ritualistic quality of the play is manifested through the use of light and sound (the police sirens), the nightly ceremony culminating in the sacrifice of a "doll-girl," abrupt changes in the tone of dialogue (Cavanosa), and the unexplained disappearances of victims' bodies. These features undermine the stability of a recognizable reality, plunging the spectator into a world of frenzy and fervor alive with the vitality of genuine spectacle. The ritual of theater, denoted by the sexual murder of women, is also linked to religion. Cavanosa's victims are made to wear a crown of thorns, so they may be blasphemously adored before they are sacrificed in order to save Cavanosa from the true nature of his own feelings toward himself, his mother, and other women. Like *Solemn Communion,* *The Grand Ceremonial,* if propitiously staged, transforms theater and its dominant emotion (love) into a religious rite which forces man to confront and reconcile his innermost conflicts and drives on an archetypal level.

IV   Le Lai de Barabbas (The Song of Barabbas)[21]

The Song of Barabbas contains many of the same motifs as *The Grand Ceremonial,* but condenses the essence of Panic in its central dramatic vision. The play relegates the theme of love and the protagonist's anguished attempt to overcome the influence of his mother to a minor plane. The nature of the Panic universe and man's role in reconciling dialectical forces within his own subconscious transcend concrete preoccupations, permitting a statement about the character of life and the creative process while uniting the audience, characters, and *mise-en-scène* in a total theater experience. The play begins with Giafar's discovery of Sylda's cadaver. Her servants, the clownlike Kardo and Malderic, appear and inform him that she can be revived by a kiss. Giafar complies and his initiation into knowledge, life and love begins. Sylda introduces him to a card game known as "The Song of Barabbas," defeating him every time they play. She informs him that she is knowledge, and that he must study philosophy to attain an understanding of the future through the laws of chance (Sylda inspires him to become a Panic man).

Sylda's alter ego, Arlys, appears to help Giafar continue his intellectual journey. The play's atmosphere becomes increasingly surreal and abstract; the characters are thousands of miles above the earth in a magical realm where time is suspended, a realm which is at once the mind of Giafar and also the universe from which he remains alienated. With the aid of Sylda's diary, Giafar traces her evolution from birth to the climactic ceremony in which she attained her state of enlightenment. Reading a document entitled *Suprème Violence,* Sylda had discovered the relationship between chance (the future, or confusion) and memory (the past). Inspired by her example and assisted by Arlys, who introduces him to the pleasures of physical love, Giafar moves toward his own initiation. Before that ceremony takes place, Arlys and Sylda fuse into a single character: Arlys-Sylda. The latter is sacrificed to a phallic knife, resurrecting the play's opening scene where Giafar found Sylda's body with a wound in the abdomen. Arlys-Sylda's mother meta-morphoses into Giafar's; after she convinces him that he hated the deceased girl and wanted to kill her (an allusion to *The Grand Cere-monial*), he undergoes the same initiation rite as did Sylda. At the play's conclusion, a knock at the door announces the arrival of a new initiate who is to discover the girl's body and begin the process just completed by Giafar.

The Song of Barabbas epitomizes a contemporary play structured around what Richard Schechner terms "life-rhythms."[22] These basic rhythms, which Schechner identifies in the theater of Beckett and Ionesco as breathing, sleeping-waking, night-day, the seasons, the phases of the moon, etc., are paralleled in Arrabal's play by the forces of reason-instinct, reality-dream and memory-chance. As Schechner states: "If these rhythms are not integrated into a career system, a form develops that has neither beginning, middle, nor end. One completed rhythm is a cycle; but the cycle ends only to begin again: nothing is resolved. . . These rhythms are a function of time. In contemporary drama, time replaces destiny. . . Life rhythms in contemporary drama make an open form of increasing tension, explosion and return to the original situation."[23] Initiation gives the play its cyclical structure, and extends Arrabal's develop-ment of a theater closely aligned to ritual and ceremony. Giafar's mentor who leads him along the path to understanding and psychic growth is of necessity a woman.[24] An analysis of the woman in both her dual aspects should provide insight into the main theme and ambience of the play as well.

Arlys and Sylda represent and embody the multifaceted qualities of woman: cruelty, poetry, mystery, illumination, repression (Sylda chains Giafar up) and liberation (Arlys enables Giafar to experience physical love). Gloria Orenstein interprets this duality in terms of the two primal influences governing Surrealist theater. Sylda's strength, violence (the ceremony), diabolical qualities, and imprisonment of Giafar suggest the cruelty derived from Artaud, while Arlys' allure, magical powers and gentle, mysterious eroticism introduce the marvelous, derived from Breton.[25] A reconciliation of the antithetical women through the Arlys-Sylda synthesis heralds the fusion of other contradictory elements occurring in the play. The sex act, in alchemical terms, also suggests a combination of opposites. The resultant androgyne provides Giafar with a more propitious perspective for dealing with life's multifaceted contradictions (underscored by Kardo and Malderic's derisive comments accompanying the love making between Giafar and Arlys which destroy love's poetic qualities).[26]

Giafar initially appears devoid of memory. He fails to appear at the appointed hour for his sexual initiation with Sylda, and he cannot recall the message he found written on her door. He finally does remember it; she wrote that she had been killed one minute after the time set for their date. When he does find her, it is in his own attic (a symbol for his mind). Arlys suggests that everything Giafar has told her may be a dream; and Sylda's diary, subtitled *"mise-en-scène,"* equates life and theater. Thus, the two aspects of woman invoke and combine two timeless conceits: life is a dream and all the world's a stage (or in Calderonian terms — "The Great Theater of the World").[27] Giafar emerges from one level of existence and ascends to a higher oneiric realm through the intervention of love which assists him to unify his vision of the dream which is life. His discovery of Arlys-Sylda's body at the end of the play confirms that the play's opening was merely a dream sequence, leaving unresolved the question of where the various realms of existence do converge.

The frontiers between reality and the dream have been completely demolished, as the dream mutated into the real, and the real was shown to be merely a dream. Through this cyclical ceremony of the derealization of reality and initiation into the norms of confusion — and later to expanded vision and integration — we realize that we are really the ones who have undergone a total aesthetic reorientation into an acceptance of the Panic universe. This is a world in which dream and reality, cruelty and the marvelous — in sum, all contradictions — can coexist in a new, expanded surreal dimension of experience."[28]

Arrabal's identification with Giafar, which helps to explain the role Giafar's parents play in his initiation, is quite clear. The father and mother, metamorphosing into Giafar's own parents rather than Sylda's, appear in symbolic form as archetypal forces affecting all mankind. The father is alternately forceful (when he rides Arlys like a horse) and ridiculous (reciting poetry while milk is being poured on his head). The mother's appearance before the final ceremony begins introduces the motif of rebirth; she forces Giafar to disassociate that part of himself represented by Arlys-Sylda and thus transcend the means (woman) of his conversion in order to attain his final objective: an understanding of the nature of reality. The mother's influence, then, explains the necessity of sacrificing Arlys-Sylda to the phallic knife; the ceremony puts Giafar in touch with his basic instincts, suppressed until this point (hence the name of the document which Giafar reads and understands: *Suprème Violence*). Like Cavanosa, Giafar desires to kill the girl who would replace his mother; but his painful struggle with internal and external forces has allowed him to progress from the adolescent stage into adulthood. His initiation allows for numerous future possibilities, suggesting psychic maturity of a much higher level than Cavanosa's.

Religion and dramatic ceremony again intermingle in *The Song of Barabbas*. The process of initiation, catalyzed by woman, begins with her offering an apple to Giafar. This motif echoes the Old Testament story of Adam and Eve (generic man and woman). The various rituals conducted by Kaldo and Malderic, contradictory in nature, culminate with the Passion of Christ. The frenzied procession to the cross, which occurs in miniature inside a bottle, is led by Sylda whose reappearance heralds Arlys' transformation into Arlys-Sylda. Life, initiation, theater, and religious rite all fuse in *The Song of Barabbas*. Their union suggests that the play may also be about the creative process itself. As Arrabal stated to Lois Messerman, both art and knowledge consist of memory and chance; both contain the same violence, the same poetic, intuitive grasp of reality: "Chance, at any given moment, determines the choice and combination of memories which constitute artistic inspiration. It is again the play of 'jeu' and 'hasard' or of order and baroque frenzy which characterizes the realized work of art which in turn is a microcosm of the universe."[29] Giafar's struggle to transcend the questions posed by ordinary reality and explore concepts such as confusion and memory mirrors Arrabal's own search for artistic inspiration. The attic is Giafar's own fantasy world, the world of dreams and the subconscious. There the author-protagonist seeks his inspiration and, as Messerman observes, "the key that unlocks this miraculous realm is that of the 'cérémonie panique' itself."[30]

The Song of Barabbas is an exercise in aesthetics, a demonstration of the possibilities for a theater totally immersed in the Panic vision. It has a didactic component, but its complex symbolism, fascinating *mélange* of images and motifs, ranging from the sublime to the grotesque, and archetypal resonances provide a universality which has at its core the human condition. Past, present, and future, birth, death, and resurrection all fuse into a resplendent whole capturing the dialectical components of the human soul in a manner at once cryptic and illuminating. As such, the play requires a staging that will immerse the audience in the dramatic milieu so that they experience its complex components in a direct and immediate fashion. *The Song of Barabbas* then develops the playwright's artistic and philosophical vision more fully than any of his previous works, confirming the dramatic possibilities of the dream world of Panic.

V   Striptease de la Jalousie (Strip Tease of Jealousy)

Striptease of Jealousy (1965), a ballet in one act, condenses themes of *The Song of Barabbas* into a short piece wich utilizes movement and dance to express emotions and communicate ideas. First, a nude female appears motionless on a stone pedestal. A man enters and examines her, first tenderly, then harshly. He puts on a record, she awakens and begins a slow, lascivious dance. She equips the man with an iron crown, a cape, and a whip. The third constituent of the piece is the group of "spectator-actors" on stage whose snickering in response to the actions of the man and woman has a strong effect on their relationship. The man dresses the girl in pants and a bra, hits her with the whip, and then caresses her tenderly. He finishes dressing her, puts handcuffs on her wrists and ankles and locks her in a spherical cage. When he takes her out to kiss her, the laughter of the "audience" enrages him and he beats her to death. He then returns her body to the stone monument, removes her clothes, and kisses her tenderly. The play concludes with his locking himself, handcuffed, into the spherical cage, and throwing the key away.

Strip Tease of Jealousy presents the diverse components of love, such as tenderness and cruelty, that coexist in all human beings. The male character fails in his struggle to dominate himself and his emotions. The spherical cage, a symbol developed more fully in several subsequent plays, represents the alchemical egg which occupies a central position in paintings of Hieronymous Bosch. In alchemical terms, the egg is the oven where baser metals are transmuted into gold; in the Surrealist vision of this playwright, it represents the union of opposites, the resolution of disparate forces and antinomies. The final act of the male affirms his isolation from the female. Their union in the egg (cage) would have allowed them to transcend themselves and fuse into an androgyne symbolic of the marvelous. The female's efforts to guide the man to that climactic union are thwarted by his jealousy.

On another level the interference of an "audience" that affects the actions of the man connotes the playwright's struggle to persuade theatergoers to exchange their traditional concept of theater for one accepting of the magical realm of the subconscious. The male's frustration echoes Arrabal's own in struggling to create a meaningful theater without having to pay heed to the "snickering" of many critics. The spectators represent both the oppressive bourgeois world referred to in such plays as *The Tricycle* and *Fando and Lis,* and the conventional theater audience also. The female dancer was inspired by the American strip tease dancer, Gypsy Rose Lee, an idol of the Surrealists.

Even though she fails to conquer the man with her movement, the male's final action does communicate the frustration he experiences upon realizing what he has lost. The Surrealist vision which the dancer represented may have amused the spectators and frustrated the male protagonist; but that vision's allure has been affirmed in the play's conclusion, and, with it, Arrabal's intention to explore further the possibilities of a theater based on the magical realm of Panic.

VI   L'Architecte et l'Empereur d'Assyrie
(The Architect and the Emperor of Assyria)

Considered by many critics to be Arrabal's finest play, *The Architect and the Emperor of Assyria* (1965) is a complex, virtuoso demonstration of the full range of dramatic possibilities of Panic. Structurally and ideologically, it develops to its absolute limit the idea of the repeating cycle, elevating this concept to a metaphysical plane reminiscent of the Argentine writer, Jorge Luis Borges.[31] Language, structure, and ritual lend a lyrical quality to this two character play which surpasses all of Arrabal's previous efforts toward creation of poetic theater. Role playing, games, and religious ritual provide much of the action of the work, establishing its tone and atmosphere. An explosion of sound and light heralds the arrival on a desert island of the Emperor of Assyria, sole survivor of a plane crash. The noise terrifies the Architect (the island's only inhabitant), a man of nature; he hides his head in the sand and responds to the Emperor's request for assistance with onomatopoeic babblings. After this very brief initial scene, the action resumes several years later. The Emperor has educated the "noble savage," instructing him in the ways of the civilized world. Their relationship is based, in part, on the diverse series of ritualistic games that they play with one another, involving domination, sado-masochism, war and death. Central to this role playing is the Emperor's agonized love-hate relationship with his mother which functions like a Wagnerian leitmotif. The first act concludes with a lengthy monologue in which the Emperor, having driven away the Architect, expresses his need for him, for God, and for his mother; during this scene he assumes the role of the other (the Architect), addressing himself to a scarecrow (the Emperor) he has placed upon his throne. The Architect returns to confirm that he is hundreds of years old.

The Architect begins the second act by playing the role of the Judge in a psychodrama evincing a fusion of reality and game. The emperor stands trial for the murder of his mother; when all the witnesses (played by the Emperor himself) have testified, he confesses his guilt and demands that he be killed and eaten by the Architect. The latter agrees and, after carrying out the cannibalistic ritual with its suggestion of the Transubstantiation, metamorphoses into the Emperor, losing his former power over the forces of nature. Just as he is exulting in his psychic self sufficiency, a crash and explosion

usher in the return of the Architect, the sole survivor of a plane-
wreck. It is now the Emperor who hides his head in the sand and
utters the identical babbling sounds made by the Architect when the
play began. The cycle has both begun and ended simultaneously in
this final image of the eternalness of man's inner conflicts and
needs.

The Architect and the Emperor of Assyria may be interpreted
from a number of perspectives. The play completes Arrabal's dramatic treatment of the figure of the mother begun in *The Two
Executioners* and *The Grand Ceremonial*. The initial image with
the airplane noises, flashes of light and explosions is suggestive of
the violent origin of man that is the birth process itself. The play's
consideration of the turmoil of man's inner life encourages a psychological analysis. Charles Lyons has utilized Jungian principles
to elucidate the thematic unity of the work. He summarizes his
overview thus: "It is possible to describe the action of *L'Architecte
et l'Empereur* as the gradual but insistent pressure of the female
unconscious forcing itself upon the male conscious mind."[32] The
play contains several references to Babylon, a city symbolic of
maternity in Jungian psychology, and to the "terrible mother of all
abominations," the receptacle of all that is wicked and unclean.[33]
Lyons identifies the primary tension in the play as the one between
the conscious (male) and the unconscious (female) mind. This central dichotomy elucidates the nature of the game structure in which
the Emperor aggressively assumes the female role.[34] The movement
of the play may then be equated with the ride to Babylon representing the ultimate sacrifice wherein the son surrenders to the mother
and is consumed by her.[35]

Two of the most striking episodes treat the theme of the mother:
the scene in which the Emperor, playing the role of a Carmelite
nun, delivers a baby; and the actual matricide confessed by the
Emperor at the climax of his trial. The former occurs near the end
of the long monologue which concludes the first act; depicting the
pain, suffering, and violence of birth, it links the parallel scenes
beginning and ending the entire drama (the plane crashes) with its
central episode and theme. In his noted production of *The Architect and the Emperor of Assyria* at the National Theater of London, Victor García utilized a visual image to relate the birth motif
to the relationship between the Emperor (civilized man) and his
"offspring," the Architect (natural man). García had the "deliv-
ery" of the Carmelite nun (portrayed by the Emperor) produce the

Architect, who rolled out from under a parachute attached to his androgynous parent by a seemingly endless umbilical cord.[36]

The cyclical repetition characteristic of myth is introduced into the description of the matricide through the striking image of the lizard emerging from the head of the Emperor's mother at the moment of her death. The reptile's face is that of the Emperor himself; the violence of birth has undergone an inversion which affirms the close psychic tie between the son and his *anima* derived directly from the mother. The lizard symbolizes the Jungian Mother-Dragon, the archetypal mother in her role as the devourer of her children. That idea is further reinforced in the following scene where the Architect implements his friend's final instructions, wearing the clothes of the Emperor's mother while eating him. After the metamorphosis of the Architect into the Emperor, the solitary Emperor is free to enjoy his independence for only a brief moment before the Architect returns to restore his psychic wholeness and resume the games they play together pantomiming the life-death-birth cycle of man.

The importance of games in Arrabal's theater has been noted from the incipience of his dramatic production. But they have never been so dominant, so all encompassing, and so central to both the themes and the dramatic structure of a play as in *The Architect and the Emperor of Assyria*. David Mendelsohn has attempted a highly original analysis of the play based upon its allusions to the game of chess.[37] For Mendelsohn, the scene where the Emperor enacts his death while dressed as the Bishop of Chess constitutes the whole play in miniature.[38] The Oedipal triangle analyzed by Lyons would then be completed by the King and Queen of chess. The motif is reinforced by the Emperor's statement that if the Architect really were his own child, he would have taught him to play chess. The game of horse and rider played by the drama's two characters suggests the Knight in chess. The intensity of competition associated with chess accounts for the play's critique on a sociological level of modern European society and its corruptive effect on the purer instincts of man (the Architect).

Mendelsohn's analysis is too complex to be summarized and evaluated here; suffice it to indicate that his utilization of the chess motif enables him to examine the mythic dimension of the play as well as identify its psychoanalytic and historical components. The play's climax has the quality of the absolute of check mate; and the role inversion at its conclusion may be viewed as the beginning of a new chess game in which the opponents have changed colors.

The accelerating rhythm of the games the two characters play and the inexorable manner in which the central conflicts of the drama emerge from even the most bizarre, pretentious and comical of those games provide the work with a rigorous, precise structure beneath the superficial chaos of its action. The Emperor cannot escape from himself; once the trial begins, the conclusion arrives rapidly as retreat and subterfuge become increasingly more difficult. The yearning of the characters for one another, or metaphorically, for psychic wholeness, functions as a musical undercurrent throughout the play. The delayed resolution of the conflict and the inexorability of its return to consciousness is suggestive of Richard Wagner's use of chromaticism in his opera, *Tristan and Isolde*.[39] Wagner's own statement about myth is striking in its relevance to *The Architect:* "In the myth, human relations almost completely lose their conventional form, which is intelligible only to the abstract reason; they show what is eternally human and eternally comprehensible in life, and show it in that concrete form, exclusive of all imitation, which gives all true myths their individual character."[40]

There is a strong bond present on both the conscious and the subconscious level between the two characters of the play. Arrabal himself speaks of the immense tenderness expressed by them, even (or perhaps, especially) in the Grand Guignolesque scene in which the Architect fulfills his promise to devour the Emperor.[41] Arrabal also suggests that the play may be a game of solitaire invented by the Emperor and that the Architect never really existed; he then adds playfully that the reverse may also be true.[42] Both possibilities permit a cohesive interpretation of the work; the nature of the characters' metamorphoses as well as the intensity of their emotions and desires reinforce their inseparability, whether they be individuals or merely aspects of a single anguished psyche seeking resolution of its schizoid existence. Dream and reality become inseparable, multilayered realms; the Architect tells of a dream in which he was alone on a desert island when a plane fell, equating Arrabal's drama with the oneiric vision of one of its characters.[43] And the Emperor affirms the possibility of physical suffering in the dream which is life. Repetition, memory, confusion and ritual[44] — essential components of the Panic vision — all combine, then, to produce and project a dramatic realm in which mutually exclusive possibilities exist and function simultaneously.

Despite Arrabal's heavy use of black humor, violent and excessive blasphemy turned ritual, and grotesqueries such as the Emperor's matricidal vision of his mother in fillets and tournedos, the poetic quality of the play still manages to dominate its style. In reviewing a production of the drama at La Mama Annex in New York City, Clive Barnes comments: "If the art of poetry is ambiguity raised to the level of either dreams or nightmares — and, by the way, it is — then this play is almost impossibly poetic."[45] Poetic theater in its broadest sense is not necessarily written in verse. Nor must it contain lyrical interludes. *The Architect* does have some marvelous passages of poetic fancy that one critic equates with Surrealist painting,[46] adding to the view of the play as a *Gesamtkunstwerk* which units the arts to serve the dramatization of myth in a manner suggestive of Wagner.

In addition to purely verbal lyricism, the play's structural rhythms produce a highly erotic sense of stage space and sufficient intensity of human feelings to sustain a genuine poetry of the theater. Norris Houghton's exposition of the nature of poetic theater could almost have been written with this play in mind. He states: "It is thanks to its articulateness that poetic drama can reveal to us our clearest glimmerings of the grandeur and dignity of the human spirit in surviving its own failure and impotence."[47] *The Architect and the Emperor of Assyria* is a play about the human spirit in unadulterated form, transcending the corruptive influence of external social and political forces. It presents that spirit both in isolation and in relationship to another; the play is at once ugly and beautiful, simple and complex, funny and tragic, optimistic and pessimistic. Precisely these paradoxes and conflicts give the work its fascination and universality. The Panic vision has been utilized in this play to provide the theater audience a glimpse into the human condition.

VII   Un chèvre sur un nuage (A Goat on a Cloud),
La jeunesse illustrée (Illustrated Youth) *and*
Dieu est-il devenu fou? (Has God Gone Mad?)

These plays, three short pieces written in 1966, utilize mime, theater space, ritualized movement and the allegorical abstraction of previous themes, motifs and characters to entrance the spectator with a visually poetic crystallization of Panic tenets.

A Goat on a Cloud is dominated by its set, a large sphere and a ladder. Much like Lira in *Guérnica*, the girl, L, is trapped in the sphere. The abstraction of Arrabal's earlier works is reflected even in the names which consist of only one letter — the initial of the name frequently utilized for most of his male (F) and female (L) protagonists. The man F struggles to extricate L. His efforts and activities are observed by a little girl who enters on a sword-horse which has two balloons attached to its handle. She forces F to climb the ladder on stage, chains him to it and laughs periodically at his words and actions. At the conclusion of the erotic dialogue between F and L, F breaks the chain, but then falls into the sphere while trying to get L out. The little girl reappears and plunges the sword she has been riding into the couple in the sphere. She laughs hysterically as bloodstained balloons rise from inside the sphere.

A Goat on a Cloud is essentially a Panic vision of love. The title evokes the god Pan (the goat), in the mist ("cloud") of confusion and obscurity. In the magical ambience of the drama, the sphere becomes a symbol of the alchemical oven where opposites are reconciled and antinomies coexist harmoniously. The hermaphrodite or androgyne becomes a central symbol of that vision. The little girl enters riding on a sword, a traditional phallic symbol. F speaks about the child (the hermaphrodite) inside his abdomen whom the woman L will help him to deliver. F unites the ideas of sexuality and intellect in the images of the stream flowing from his penis to his brain and a drop of blood emanating from his brain which is transformed into a white viscous liquid (sperm). Body and mind, the cerebral and the corporal, the male and the female, all merge in the magical sphere which is the symbol central to the Panic world. The little girl who appears in Arrabal's first Panic play, *Solemn Communion,* returns to assert her liberation from the restrictive norms of society. Her final act encapsulates the ambiguity and confusion central to the play; it is a ritual sacrifice, much like that in *The Song of Barabbas*, affirming the potency of the phallic knife (sexuality), but also being a wanton, irrational act of erotic violence destroying an amorous couple. Love's dialectic is potically captured in this cryptic depiction of human thoughts and feelings ordered by the precise logic inherent in the Panic vision.

Illustrated Youth demonstrates the effect of the forces of time and memory on a previous work, *Fando and Lis*. It further abstracts the earlier play, already set in a dramatic world removed from everyday reality. As the work begins, a man is reading a book entitled *The Relativity of Time*. That book serves as an announcement of the play's principal thematic focus. The man hides as a boy and girl appear. The boy and girl are passionately in love according to the same pattern seen in *Fando and Lis*. The girl, who is referred to only as She, solicits increasingly cruel behavior from the boy, He. While He is beating her on the foot with nettles, the man attempts to intervene and is struck by the boy, with a rock. There is a blackout on stage; when the lights are brought back up, one senses that a great deal of time has passed. An old woman appears wearing the same clothes that the young girl had worn. She sees the man who has revived from the blow he received and implores him nostalgically to chain her to the tree and beat her on the foot with nettles as her own lover had done sixty years before.

The mutliplicity of events and people is suggested by the boy's amorous description of the girl's two right and three left hands that are "white like six hundred divine comedies" and whose fingers are "constellations of miniscule landing fields for helicopters and exterminating angels."[48] The boy and girl appear larger than life and the cyclical pattern of their relationship further enhances the mythic quality of the work. Arrabal's Panic vision of love incorporates Nietzsche's concept of "eternal return" and a compression of time that ruptures the chronology of waking reality. *Fando and Lis* has become a Panic myth eternalizing a dialectical view of love which combines tenderness, lyricism and compassion with pain and suffering.

Has God Gone Mad? is a mime play which utilizes music, laughter, and rhythmical changes in the stage position of the actors to reflect — in a Panic manner — the meaninglessness of life under an insane god. The couple, A and M, begin the action playing on flutes like snake charmers, thereby summoning B and N from a house. The two men and women alternate sitting on the shoulders of the person of the same sex in response to drum rolls originating inside the house. The house appears to represent the oppressive forces of the world; reprobative noises and mocking laughter emanating from inside destroy the joy and sensuality shared by the two couples. After all four appear on the ground crying, one pair manages to rise and enter the house; a pair of flutes then emerges magically from inside the house which the remaining couple uses to play the music beginning the drama.

Has God Gone Mad? ritualizes the fruitlessness of man's endeavors to give meaning to life through human empathy and love. The title and dramatic movement of the play is reminiscent of Albert

Camus' projection in his essay, "The Myth of Sisyphus," of the absurdity of life. Arrabal's brief work condenses into a few basic movements time and the full range of human emotions. The Panic writer visualizes a macrocosmos controlled by a malicious or insane god opposed to all human joy. He depicts the confining nature of existence through the use of symmetry in his art, striking out at this evil god through both the content and the dramatic structure of his work. The confusion, uncertainly, and persisting hope found in life is condensed in the questionmark of the play's title. Arrabal's experiment with nonverbal drama is difficult to evaluate without having had the opportunity to experience its effect in the theater. It appears, however, that Panic does lend itself to visual representation. *Has God Gone Mad?* is a minor work, but one that is fascinating and disturbing to an audience.

VIII   Le Jardin des delices (The Garden of Delights)

Written in 1967 after release from prison in Spain, *The Garden of Delights* combines autobiographical elements with an exploration of the possibilities for psychological liberation from confining past memories and present self doubts. The central character in this Panic ceremony is the actress, Laïs. In what appears to be the present, Laïs is being interviewed for a television program via the telephone. She has cut herself off from the outside world, living, with her nine sheep, in the company of the ape-like Zenon, who is in love with her. The dramatic action oscillates between the past and the present. Two characters, Teloc and Miharca, seem to represent Laïs' past; they appear whenever the actress' neuroses, memories and anxieties summon them. Teloc and Miharca play a number of roles, revealing the traumatic feelings and memories in Laïs' subconscious that influence her present thoughts and actions. When Teloc and Miharca penetrate the barrier between the past and the present a dramatic catharsis results in which Laïs murders Miharca. She then instructs Zenon to devour the jar of jelly which contains the actress' soul. When he does so, he acquires the stature of a true human being and joins her in an ecstatic union in the egg derived from Hieronymous Bosch's painting "The Garden of Earthly Delights."

The spectator's orientation in time is continually challenged and disturbed in this work; sounds (the telephone), lighting, and images on a screen combine to release the audience from the restraints of ordinary chronology. Miharca's and Teloc's appearances and role playing exteriorize timeless psychic forces harbored in man's subconscious. They function both to interject a note of mystery and magic (essential features of the drama's ambience) and to unite those elements with autobiographical concerns and details.

The metaphysical prison restraining the artist (Arrabal-Laïs) and the horror of the dramatist's actual incarceration in Spain fuse in the hallucinatory scene in which Laïs visualizes her torture by Teloc. This highly traumatic fantasy shows the magician Teloc in the dual role of oppressor and spiritual master; his cruel acts oblige Laïs to confess the truth about her past and deal with it in the context of present reality. The concept of reality acquires added meaning in the light of Arrabal's analysis of his imprisonment as a rebirth, a return to the womb and a rediscovery of his father.[49] The author's identification with a female character becomes meaningful when Laïs exchanges her identity with Zenon, a symbol of pure masculine passion. This androgynous union is an affirmation of the gentle, artistic component of man combined with the violent sexual nature derived from the father. As Lois Messerman has perceptively noted: "*The Garden of Delights* depicts androgyne not only in its visibly erotic forms but in its symbolic significance as the reintegration of disparate and longing facets of the self, the very force we have seen at work in Arrabal's dramatic universe."[50]

The egg is a key symbol in the play; it unites Arrabal's artistic vision with Bosch's. Because the egg plays a central role in that painter's famous tryptich, "The Garden of Earthly Delights," it functions as an announcement of the importance of visual elements in the play. The music and stage movement at the beginning of the second act anticipate the final climactic union of Zenon and Laïs. Zenon appears carrying a huge egg; its top is open, and it is covered with scenes from Bosch's painting. Zenon then pulls Laïs roughly into the egg; their lovemaking inside is interrupted by a policeman investigating Miharca's disappearance. The egg, the erotic nature of the scene with Zenon, and the intriguing image accompanying it — of a boat carrying a tree upon which a bird is perched with its beak padlocked — all demonstrate the potential for unrestrained artistic expression that will come when the magical language of the Panic ceremony is liberated.[51] The atmosphere of the drama is pervaded by the fascinating perversity of Bosch's painting. The use of slide projections, of sense disorientation (Teloc's magic helmet), and lighting effects underscores the violence, horror, and charm of the Panic world. It is as if "Paradise" and "Hell," the outer panels of Bosch's tryptich, were united in Arrabal's dramatic vision to form an actual Garden of Earthly Delights, an uneasy union of dualities that has come to characterize the dramatist's theater ceremonies.

In an important sequence of the play, Miharca's return in the present time as a madwoman bent on discrediting Teloc becomes the climax of a series of dazzling visual stimuli.[52] She is a figure from Bosch's hell, a temptress whose power over Laïs and her past, based in part on their mutual sexual experimentation (real or fantasized), is reminiscent of the domination exerted over Arrabal by his mother. Teloc exposes Miharca's love-hate relationship with Laïs; only when Miharca is ritually sacrificed to the phallic knife symbolic of masculine sexuality is Laïs truly free. At that moment, her sheep, which had jealously been slaughtered by Zenon, are restored to life. Their presence balances the violence of erotic passion with the tenderness of spiritual live. Having integrated love's dialectic, Laïs is now able to join Zenon in the egg, throw away the key (unlocking the beak of the bird in the boat and enabling his song of freedom to be heard) and to ascend to personal and artistic liberation.

By making Laïs an actress, Arrabal is able to express feelings about art and life which unite those entities in a single vision. Laïs seeks freedom from the repressions of her religious schooling through theater just as Arrabal himself has done. Both author and character have struggled to transcend a host of imprisoning memories. In *The Garden of Delights,* Laïs is an actress playing the role of an actress; the idea of levels of dream and reality is thereby communicated. Liberation and self affirmation are achieved only when the distinction between theater and life has been blurred to the point of eradication.

The union of opposites has been shown to be an essential feature of Panic. It manifests itself in this play in the dialectical view of love, while the play's final image, the alchemical union in the egg, incorporates the work's climactic duality, combining the violence and tenderness of love, the synthesis of male and female, of art and life, and of heaven and hell into a single vision. This vision liberates both author and audience from the confines of chronological time and of past events, converting memory into a creative rather than a restrictive force.

IX   Ars Amandi (The Art of Love)

Arrabal's *Ars Amandi,* written during 1967–1968, explores more fully the theme of love within the context of the Panic theater ceremony. The lyrical structure of *The Architect and the Emperor of Assyria* and the importance of visual elements noted in *The Garden of Delights* are combined and developed even further in this drama. *Ars Amandi* is subtitled "Opéra Panique" ("Panic Opera"); virtually all of the dialogue is sung, confirming the growing importance of music in Arrabal's theater; the rhythms, harmonies and dissonances detected in *The Architect* on an abstract level are accorded a more direct musical expression in *Ars Amandi.* The Panic ceremony and its ambience emerge as the magical realm of the human mind, their sublimity and baseness communicated by a union of the arts.

The initial (and final) image of *Ars Amandi* presents the generic woman, Lys, as a giantess covered by swarms of insects, ultimately revealed to be the souls of men. The protagonist Fridigan is searching for his lost friend, Erasmus Marx. He encounters the giantess Lys, and sees her transformed magically, like Alice in Wonderland, into a normal-sized woman. She is copying the word OUI (yes) on a canvas, but her model says NON (no). Fridigan's lengthy, painful search for his friend puts him in contact with Lys' stuttering servants, Bana and Ang. They are fluent only when they sing; out of deference to them Lys sings also. Fridigan follows suit, justifying the operatic mode of the work. Fridigan encounters mannequins representing such myths as Frankenstein, Dracula, and King Kong (fear and horror); Tom Thumb and Pinocchio (childhood innocence); Romeo (undying love); Othello (jealous passion); Tarzan (primitive or natural man); Faust (the quest for knowledge); and Christ and Don Quixote (idealized, self sacrificing *agape*). Fridigan is forced to tolerate the seemingly irrational changes in mood and behavior of Lys and her servants, accept verbal and physical abuse from them, and recognize and deal with his own emotions. Finally he is ready to participate in the climactic ceremony affirming the dialectical nature of love. He consents to undergo surgery (physically and metaphorically) at the hand of Lys, then joins Erasmus Marx as one of the insects on her again enlarged body.

Ars Amandi makes greater use of the arts than any of Arrabal's previous works. As an opera libretto the work demands a musical score; its lyric character is further reinforced by the precisely ordered repetitions of motifs, poetic passages, and even entire scenes[53] which impart a rhythmic quality to the drama. As Gloria Orenstein has commented: "In this musical spectacle, the themes and images studied in the earlier works are combined contrapuntally in a fugal treatment, in which the mathematically precise composition serves as the framework for the expression in stage imagery of the total Panic confusion on all levels of art and experience."[54] The use of slides and the projection of other visual images become an integral component of the aesthetic of the play while also contributing to its theme. Etchings by Goya and paintings by Bosch and by Max Ernst as well as one designed and commissioned by Arrabal himself[55] combine with the use of props and even the physical position of the characters to evoke the plastic arts.[56]

This assault on the senses of the audience evinces the influence of Artaud; the allusions to the sky falling and to surgery may also be linked to him.[57] The operation performed on Fridigan by Lys symbolizes the spiritual transformation effected by the theatrical ceremony in the audience and protagonist. Fridigan, whose name alludes to the frigidity of his spiritual and physical being prior to this "transformation," is able to achieve a more meaningful level of existence through physical and metaphysical suffering. Lys' aloofness and frequent rejection of him are more painful than the beatings he suffers at the hands of Bana and Ang, psychic projections of his inner turmoil which cannot be articulated (the servants' stuttering) or comprehended in the context of ordinary, rather than Panic existence. The attacks upon his spirit that help to effect his conversion are mirrored by the play's assault on the senses and psyche of the audience. The climax of the drama, as Ms. Orenstein has so perceptively stated, "is a veritable spiritual transformation, in which our consciousness has been expanded, so that the original image of the play, when seen at the end, has a new, hallucinated meaning for the spectator. This is Arrabal's visual yardstick to measure the transformation of humanity's vision."[58]

The central aesthetic of the play may also be related to its principal theme. The grotesque is an artistic mode which achieves its impact because of its dialectical nature. The union of opposites which, in the case of the grotesque are the comic and the horrifying, is a central component of the Panic vision. Their reconciliation and synthesis are essential if the higher reality, which is at once the Panic world, the "Garden of Delights," and the magical realm of alchemy, is to be attained. The initial image of Lys copying the word NO by painting YES announces the essential role of conflicting forces in the play. That idea is reingforced throughout the work. The visual image of Lys bearing Ang on her shoulders while Bana kneels before her kissing her abdomen reflects the duality of love that is its very essence. Fridigan's declaration of love to Lys further reinforces this concept; he calls her "my labyrinth of fascinations and of repugnances" (p. 58). Those words are echoed by a sensorial oxymoron in the form of stage directions calling for "a thousand butterflies to cross the stage with the noise of tanks" (p. 58).

The primal image, however, serving to unite the aesthetic of the grotesque with the theme of love is found near the end of the play. Before accepting Fridigan's love, Lys commands him to wallow in the mud with pigs. They shower excrement upon him and she joins him in the mire. Photos of slaughter houses, restaurants featuring gastronomical delicacies garnished with a pig's head, daisies, and paintings by Joan Miró are all flashed on a screen. The repugnant and the beautiful coalesce in a dazzling display at once humorous, repulsive, and moving. In order to attain paradise through love, it is first necessary to pass through the basest of realms. The violence and cruelty inherent in genuine eroticism, present throughout the play, are united with its tender component. Fridigan is free to accept even death at Lys' hand; the final image uniting him and Marx has been produced through the mediation of a woman. And Lys' return to enormity affirms the mythic nature of his experience.

The mannequins in the play also serve to impart a mythical quality to it. They help Fridigan empathize with and understand human suffering and sacrifice by miming the story of Christ. Paradoxically, however, their performance moves him only when done as a grotesque parody utilizing role reversals so that Tarzan takes the part of Christ and King Kong is Mary Magdalene. This mini-ceremony, like the full scale theater ceremony *Ars Amandi* is, achieves its effect through the utilization of a dialectical aesthetic mode (the grotesque) to produce conflicting emotions in the audience. Like *The Architect and the Emperor of Assyria, Ars Amandi* is a total art work suggesting the Wagnerian *Gesamtkunstwerk.*

In analyzing one of Wagner's favorite myths, the Tristan and Isolde legend, Denis de Rougemont makes a statement about myth in general which helps to illuminate Arrabal's aesthetic and ideology in this play. He says: "A myth arises whenever it becomes dangerous or impossible to speak plainly about certain social or religious matters, or affective relations, and yet there is a desire to preserve these or else it is impossible to destroy them ... a myth is needed to express the dark and unmentionable fact that passion is linked with death, and involves the destruction of anyone yielding himself up to it with all his strength."[59] Arrabal does not "speak plainly" about love, life and art; instead he creates a magical language utilizing a diverse range of art forms which, when comprehended, enrich the inner life of the initiate. By deciphering that language, the spectator is free to join Fridigan and Erasmus Marx (socio-political forces concretized and humanized) in celebrating a spiritual apotheosis. The concluding celebration takes the form of a Negro revival meeting complete with handclapping and the joyous singing of spirituals. The author's presence is strongly felt; Arrabal has reason to rejoice because he has liberated himself, through his theater, from the psychological pain which formerly imbued his treatment of love. In *Ars Amandi,* he affirms eroticism and its positive role in life in a manner exuding optimism.

X   Bestialité érotique (Erotic Bestiality)

Erotic Bestiality, written in 1968, constitutes a climactic affirmation of the force of eroticism; for that reason it is a logical sequel to *Ars Amandi.* A shorter, simpler play, *Erotic Bestiality* juxtaposes the dark humor of the grotesque with a lyrical, uplifting expression of human sensuality. As Franco Tonelli has so aptly noted, the play "gives dramatic life to eroticism in its absolute purity without the interference of any moral, psychological or sociological contingency dissipating its primal essence."[60]

As the play begins, Asan enters mounted on a mare played by an actress. Alima then appears on a steed in the form of an actor. While the "horses" engage in erotic activity to the extent that their harnesses permit, Asan and Alima speak of their love for one another. Their amorous declarations take the form of coarse, salacious insults in which each ecstatically extols the ugliness and repulsiveness of the other. This section of the play reaches its climax in a perverse display of sexuality in which Asan and Alima frenetically lick the soles of each other's shoes. In a central mimed episode, a ship in the form of a fish descends from above, and the two horses depart in it to the accompaniment of operatic music and falling flower petals. The final scene demonstrates a completely different tone from the earlier part of the work. The dialogue between Asan and Alima becomes extremely lyrical; their expressions of love are now tender and poetic. The skeletons of the two horses fall from above, and the lovers embrace at the play's conclusion.

Erotic Bestiality is a play based on paradoxes, wit and poetry. The title itself is ironic in light of the fact that the drama contains one of the most tender and lyrical love scenes in all of Arrabal's theater. The dualistic nature of love is communicated here in a more direct and immediate fashion than in previous plays. The dominant note in the first and longer section of the work, however, is its scabrous humor. The aesthetic governing that portion of the drama is the grotesque. As Asan and Alima's passion grows in intensity, each one's affirmations of the ugliness and loathesomeness of the other become increasingly more extravagant in nature.[61] Alima even repudiates Asan for loving her exclusively for her ugliness. This inverted expression of passion mimics and mocks the traditional language of love, and is juxtaposed with the more genuine eroticism of the two horses. Just as Fridigan had to pass through the mire in order to attain the celestial heights of Panic life, Asan and Alima must first recognize and give expression to basic feelings in their purest form.[62] Once they have done so, they become free to experience also the rapturous delights resulting from the union of two spirits in love. Arrabal appears to have reconciled the contradictory components of love in his own mind; the play's final section is replete with images referring to sand and the sea, motifs associated in the author's mind with Melilla and his father. By accepting the presence of the father image in his own psyche, Arrabal succeeds in giving himself free reign to express poetically the allure and incandescence of untrammeled human passion.

XI Une tortue nommée Dostoievski
(A Tortoise Named Dostoievsky)

A Tortoise Named Dostoievsky, written in 1968 and inspired by Arrabal's reading of Dostoievsky's *The Crocodile,* is a play which projects the joy and fulfillment its author has found in Panic tempered by resonances of his imprisonment in Spain and his anguished concern over his wife's health.[63] The plot is extremely simple: Liska and Malik visit the zoo where they examine the giant radioactive tortoise, with its head of a lion, that was the product of a nuclear war. In his excitement, Malik gets too close to the somnolent creature and is swallowed by it. Unharmed inside, Malik experiences a sort of rebirth there, has visions of paradise, and is ultimately joined in his new realm by Liska and the animal's caretaker, Papiri, who has become Don Quixote.

A *Tortoise Named Dostoievsky* is an expression on one level of the author-protagonist's Oedipal yearnings. Malik's residence inside the tortoise suggests a return to the womb. But that return is not synonymous with a surrender to the force of the mother. The return becomes instead a sort of renaissance effected by the presence of the father. Malik had related his own paternal desires to Liska, experienced as a dream. The idea of the father is reinforced by Malik's vision of the absent parent while inside the tortoise.[64] The interior of the creature also suggests the prison cell where Arrabal rediscovered his own father and experienced what he has described as a psychic rebirth.[65] The final union with Liska inside the tortoise is reminiscent of the ascension to Panic paradise, also effected by love, in *The Garden of Delights*.

Here, however, the liberation of the protagonist is achieved not only through a female intermediary, but also because of a new political awareness. Among Malik's visions of the past experienced in the magical realm inside the tortoise is the French Revolution. Reference to a nuclear war interjects another political note. The magical sphere where the two lovers are united is revealed to be the world of the marvelous; the projection of Bosch's paintings and of scenes from *Alice in Wonderland* helps to identify it as such. The final note uniting artistic creativity with political *engagement* is the appearance of Don Quixote who represents the ideal of political freedom and the need to "right wrongs" in both a Spanish and a universal context. A *Tortoise Named Dostoievsky* then is a play affirming both the allure and efficacy of an aesthetic based on the magical ambience of Panic. It also announces the author's intention to deal with political themes and realities in subsequent endeavors.

XII   Une Orange sur le Mont de Venus
(An Orange on Venus' Mountain)

Written in 1968 but not published until 1976, *An Orange on*

Venus' Mountain is a very short work utilizing several of Arrabal's favorite theatrical devices to explore the nature of love and the reconciliation of its dialectical components. As the play begins, Lois is locked in a cage, naked. Goya, wearing the costume of an animal trainer in a circus, has Lois perform for the audience. He speaks to her harshly and insultingly, using his circus whip unsparingly. She carries out his orders subserviently, even eating a bug on command. He informs the crowd that he abducted her from the Nordic country where she was a member of the royal family. When it is time to perform her climactic trick, Lois hesitates, but soon acquiesces to Goya's tyrannical insistence. While she lies perfectly still on a table, he slices an orange in half and squeezes the juice on her genital area. He then asks for a volunteer from the audience to come and lick up the liquid; Lois is not to move or even to blink during the process. When her eyes do move, Goya becomes furious; he threatens her with all sorts of dire punishments; and finally brands her between the breasts with a hot iron. She begs his forgiveness, affirming that she is his slave. He looks at her winsomely, embracing her while rapturously declaring his love for her. He then tells her to don his circus uniform. When she does so, her entire demeanor changes. She strikes him with the whip and announces the beginning of another show, using the same words Goya had spoken earlier.

An Orange on Venus' Mountain is a performance within a performance constituting a miniature repository of Arrabalian dramatic techniques. The play's atmosphere reflects the magical charm and confusion of the Panic ceremony. The work underscores Arrabal's fondness for antinomies: love is shown to be cruel and tender, violent and gentle. Sadism and masochism, as Arrabal has stated in numerous interviews, are natural components of eroticism rather than sexual perversions. The sexual act, symbolized by Venus, the goddess of love, results in the production of the androgynous being who resolves and embodies those dualities. The mountain of the title is a Freudian symbol for the male sex organ;[66] but it is also the abode of Venus, whose femininity is suggested by the orange, a common symbol for the female breast. The orange, on one level, introduces a note of incongruous humor in the play, but its circular shape signifies the cyclical nature of the play's structure and also suggests the cycles occurring in erotic relationships. In Freudian terms, the title projects us into the future when, at the end of another cycle, the orange will be squeezed over the male sex organ (the mountain). Goya, the Panic artist (as indicated by his name), creates a central image revealing him to be the subject of his own work. The act of infusing Lois, the "cold" Nordic princess, with warmth and love inspires the creative artist to express himself with renewed vitality.

The role reversal, given the character traits of Goya and Lois, recalls Lasca and Tiossido's switch in *The Car Cemetery*. But the integration of the metamorphosis in *An Orange on Venus' Mountain,* with its theme and structure, elevates its role to a higher plane reminiscent of *The Architect and the Emperor of Assyria. An Orange on Venus' Mountain* constitutes a remarkable example of Arrabal's ability to summarize and condense dramatic concerns and techniques into a short piece which, though lacking the depth of major Panic works, is still engaging and moving both on a visual and an intellectual level.

Arrabal's Panic period proved to be pivotal in his career as a dramatist. The years 1960-1968 witnessed the recognition of his talents throughout the world. He authored several of his finest works, most notably *The Architect and the Emperor of Assyria* and *The Garden of Delights*, during this time. The Panic Movement gave unity to his dramatic production and allowed him to broaden his concept of theater. His utilization of slides, music, visual images, and lighting effects resulted in a form of total theater that realized more fully than perhaps any other dramatist's work the theories of Antonin Artaud expressed in his famous collection of manifestos, "The Theater and Its Double."[67] Surrealist techniques and concerns played a major role in shaping his idea of theater based on Panic. But Arrabal's imprisonment and direct contact with the horror of political oppression led to a need to reexamine his role as a playwright and artist in the context of current socio-political forces in *The Garden of Delights, Erotic Bestiality,* and *A Tortoise Named Dostoievsky.* The magical realm of Panic is at once a refuge from mundane reality and an aesthetic device allowing the author to consider pragmatic human concerns in a more direct and forceful manner.

The Panic Movement, if it is a movement, really began with a number of Arrabal's plays which predated its formal initiation. Concomitantly, the Movement's termination was not abrupt or absolute. Subsequent works utilized similar techniques but, beginning with the plays, *L'Aurore rouge et noire (The Red and Black Dawn,* 1968) and *Et ils passèrent des menottes aux fleurs (And*

They Put Handcuffs on the Flowers, 1969), a shift in emphasis is clearly detectable. The politically committed and aware playwright was then to utilize what was already a mature and highly developed dramatic technique to explore subjectively the segment of objective reality now attracting and demanding his full attention.

CHAPTER 4

A New Theater of Politics

A LL literature reflects to some degree the society in which it is
produced; in analyzing a literary work, the critic should be
sensitive to the socio-political forces shaping its form and aesthetic.
Certain works of literature encourage and facilitate a particular
critical approach. Proponents of the sociological or Marxist school
seek to define both the nature and the function of a literary work in
terms of socio-political currents. In his essay, "The Sociology of
Theater," Georges Gurvitch applies the tenets of sociological criticism to the genre of theater in the following manner: "The theater
is a sublimation of certain social situations, whether it idealizes
them, parodies them, or calls for them to be transcended. The
theater is simultaneously a sort of escape hatch from social conflicts and the embodiment of those conflicts."[1]

The early plays of Fernando Arrabal incorporate Gurvitch's concept of theater.[2] Despite the overall subordination of their socio-
political dimension to psychological concerns, the childlike characters of those plays embody the social conflicts that they seek but
generally fail to escape. In the dramas of his Panic period, Arrabal
has expanded significantly the philosophical base for his theater
and enriched the aesthetic techniques utilized in projecting his
vision of life. The presence of social forces in that magical, oneiric
ambience is undeniable, however; they constitute a subtle undercurrent periodically rupturing the atmosphere of ordered confusion
characteristic of the Panic ceremony. And in plays like *Solemn
Communion, The Architect and the Emperor of Assyria,* and *The
Garden of Delights,* these forces fuse with and at times even dominate psychological and aesthetic concerns.

Although Arrabal's theater of these first two periods did contain
a significant socio-political component, his experiences as a prisoner in Spain in 1967 and as a participant in the May, 1968, student

rebellion in Paris had a profound effect immediately reflected in his work. In a sense, they forced him to emerge from the "escape hatch" of the Panic vision to confront the realities of political oppression in a much more direct manner. The plays written after those experiences began to exhibit a new didactic orientation. Arrabal's early theater had served a therapeutic purpose; but he no longer felt such a strong need to wrestle with his own psychological conflicts on stage or to identify strongly with his protagonists. This is not to say that all previous concerns and aesthetic techniques were abandoned. Role playing, dreams and nightmares, biographical motifs, the tenets of Panic, parody and grotesque deformation continued to figure prominently in his theater. But the new direction of his drama was undeniable and, of necessity, was accompanied by a corollary expansion in stage technique. Arrabal's evolving sense of visual detail caused him to experiment with innovative devices within the theater and also to turn to the cinema where he could transcend the physical limitations of the stage and implement some of his ideas more efficaciously. These changes in the playwright's orientation demand a concomitant shift in critical approach. Psychological analysis would no longer prove fruitful, while a sociological orientation would be productive. Knowledge of politics in Spain and throughout the world is basic to understanding allusions in Arrabal's more recent works.

The broadening of Arrabal's dramatic vision and the didactic intent of his work attenuate his ability to fascinate and frighten an audience by enveloping them in the bizarre and unsettling world of his dreams and obsessions. In more inspired works, such as *Sur le Fil (On the Wire*, 1974), the best features of his Panic period combine with his new-found political commitment to produce an outstanding work of the theater. Other plays, however, suffer from a lack of cohesion and a diminution of the dramatist's unique ability to disorient and intrigue his audience. But even Arrabal's weakest plays exhibit a wonderful sense of visual imagery, sensitivity to theater space and a provocative utilization of satire and humor.

The general tone for this period of Arrabal's dramatic writing is established by the transitional work, *L'Aurore rouge et noire (The Red and Black Dawn,* 1968), and its more highly developed and complex sequel, *And They Put Handcuffs on the Flowers* (1969). These works, inspired directly by Arrabal's incarceration in Spain and contact with the May revolution in Paris, exhibit the weaknesses of his didactic works while still managing, particularly in the latter play, to provide a total theater experience which in its more inspired moments is telling and poetic.

I L'Aurore rouge et noire (The Red and Black Dawn)

The Red and Black Dawn consists of four short plays published together with *And They Put Handcuffs on the Flowers* in a volume entitled *Théâtre Guerilla (Guerrilla Theater)*. The stage directions allow for the works to be performed either in the street (where a corral is to be constructed utilizing enormous photographs to enclose the space) or in a conventional theater. The plays as a group exhibit some features of guerrilla or street theater; but Arrabal's blending of sexuality and politics into an artistic whole where dream and reality have fused makes of that theatrical subgenre something uniquely his own.

The first play, *Groupuscule de mon coeur (The Groupuscule of My Heart),*[3] communicates Arrabal's view of the struggle of the students and workers in Paris in 1968 as the continuation of the eternal and universal battle against injustice and oppression. A Roman torture wheel and a drummer's gothic costume constitute visual symbols projecting that idea. The somewhat rhetorical dialogue of the revolutionaries alternates with mimed action centering around a woman turning the wheel, a uniformed figure, and an amorous young couple. The uniformed man suppresses the other characters' attempts at expressing themselves through love and art (the playing of a violin); he finally places a crown of thorns on the heads of the young couple. When the revolutionaries abandon their stilted rhetoric and decide to enjoy themselves, throwing the money around raised for an undetermined purpose, the woman pushing the wheel reveals that the uniformed man has become a skeleton. The young couple rejoices, and the woman hoists a red flag in jubilant celebration.

The Groupuscule of My Heart is a relatively simple, direct condemnation of all oppression, symbolized by the wheel and the silent uniformed man. His repressive actions are reminiscent of those in *The Condemned Man's Bicycle*. Freedom of sexual expression is linked to political freedom throughout the play; their union is finalized in a statement made by the *Enragé:* "We will unbutton our minds as frequently as we do our flies."[4] The play is simplistic, as guerrilla theater must be, yet Arrabal introduces a lyrical note through images, both verbal (the title) and visual, enabling the piece to transcend the purely polemical.

Tous les parfums d'Arabie (All the Perfumes of Arabia) also contains its central poetic image in its title. The action takes place in present day Spain, a land seeped in blood whose internal rotting has produced an odor that cannot be eradicated by all the perfumes of Arabia. The play is based on an actual event: the execution of Juilán Grimau for "crimes" committed in the Civil War twenty-four years before. The central visual image is a huge white cloth stained with blood which drips into a basin underneath. Ybar (Grimau) has been sentenced to death; his wife, Maida, seeks to have his sentence commuted. She pleads with Franco's personal confessor, with a general and with a banker, but all spout the official rhetoric of the regime in power and "graciously" decline to help. Each washes his hands in the basin of blood after concluding the conversation. At the play's conclusion Ybar is executed and Maida comes to express her grief and decorously covers the body of her husband.

All the Perfumes of Arabia is a simple work, structured in time by a pendulum which ticks off the minutes of life remaining to the prisoner. Ybar is the quintessential revolutionary, and the three dignitaries, all played by the same actor (thus exposing the complicity of church, state and capital in the dictatorship) are stereotypes satirized by the playwright. The play conforms closely to the standard view of guerrilla theater both in technique and effect. It is simplistic and — for Arrabal — unimaginative; but as a didactic piece succeeds in making its impact.

Sous les pavés, la plage (Under the Stones, the Beach) fails as guerrilla theater because of the dramatist's attempt to incorporate a perverse eroticism (better suited to a psychologically oriented play like *The Grand Ceremonial*) into his affirmation of the revolutionary spirit. Photos of students and police and shouted orders for the construction of barricades intermingle with mimed scenes involving two women and a young man. The violence of revolution infiltrates the erotic relationship of the trio. The young man is crowned with a bizarre headgear in the style of Bosch which covers his eyes and bound and gagged by two women who treat him first roughly and then tenderly. The portrayal of eroticism in the piece emphasizes its dialectical nature in a manner reminiscent of earlier plays like *The Song of Barabbas* and *Ars Amandi*. As the trio's activity reaches its climax, the young man is fed the ears and breasts one of the women has cut off the other. This action is set against a drummer's narration of the courage of the students. With the noise in the background of pounding boots, the young man is carried forth in a *sedia gestatoria* covered by a giant ear. Under the stones (symbolic of the violence of revolt) is the beach, Arrabal's symbol for his father whom he equates with liberty in both a sexual and a political context. The playwright has sought to force too much into this short play and, as a result, the work fails to achieve its purpose.

Les fillettes (The Boxes) is a short, effective work of guerrilla theater. It affirms the brotherhood of all mankind — represented by political prisoners from around the world — while characters, who cannot communicate because of the language barrier, join together in singing the "Internationale" from their respective cages. The plight of Karin, a Greek prisoner, is made far more moving by the depiction in a dream sequence of the blissful love he shares with a French student, Lia. Arrabal's hope for the freedom of the oppressed everywhere emerges triumphant at the play's conclusion when the image of the brutally murdered Karin, just as in the legend of Saint Veronica and Christ, remains imprinted on the handkerchief Lia uses to wipe his face.

The Red and Black Dawn is by no means an important piece of dramatic literature.[5] At times, as in *Under the Stones, the Beach,* it suffers from pretentiousness and diffuseness that negate its purpose. However, some moments of poetic tenderness are genuinely moving. In *All the Perfumes of Arabia* and *The Cages,* Arrabal's methodology is entirely appropriate; the plays are clear and to the point, attaining an artistic level above that of the typical guerrilla play. *The Red and Black Dawn* establishes the fundamental direction a number of Arrabal's subsequent plays will follow. It exhibits a heightened didactic intent, but seeks also to incorporate the author's aesthetic. *And They Put Handcuffs on the Flowers* adopts some of the content as well as the basic approach of these plays, but develops guerrilla theater into a complex dramatic form providing a unique total theater experience.

II   Et ils passèrent des menottes aux fleurs
(And They Put Handcuffs on the Flowers)

In an interview during the New York production of *And They Put Handcuffs on the Flowers,* Arrabal stated that "theater should be very intense. For the audience it should be dangerous and revelatory."[6] And the drama *Handcuffs* should "be thought of as a shout."[7] Seeking to respond to the horrors encountered in Spanish prisons by providing the theater audience with an intense experience, Arrabal includes specific stage directions at the beginning of *Handcuffs* aimed at eliminating the traditional actor-audience opposition. The spectators are to be plunged into the oppressive milieu of Spain and its prisons even before the drama begins; they are to be accosted, separated from their companions, verbally and physically abused by the actors, and ultimately encouraged to participate directly in the performance.[8] Audience involvement, the use of character stereotypes denoted by masks and hats, and direct narration of socio-political abuses in Fascist Spain combine to produce a unique form of guerrilla theater.

The action proper begins in the interior of a Spanish prison. The drama is structured in a manner similar to *Ars Amandi;* grotesque scenes alternate with poignant ones, the tone of the work frequently shattered by violent excesses contained in dream sequences. The first part presents three prisoners, Amiel, Kator and Pronos,[9] incarcerated for over twenty years. The sadism and hypocrisy of the Spanish Church and its officials are manifested in the realms of dream and reality; both emerge ultimately as components of the unified nightmare that is life in Spain. The human feelings and weaknesses of the prisoners are expressed in their sexual fantasies engendered by physical and emotional deprivations they have suffered.

Much of the play's structure is based on the dream-reality dichotomy; the latter portion of the work, however, derives its structure from a more conventional device. After Tosan arrives, the drama essentially reproduces the short play, *All the Perfumes of Arabia.* Tosan, like Ybar, is inspired by the Spaniard, Julián Grimau. His execution occurs despite efforts of his devoted wife to have his sentence commuted. The same props employed in the earlier piece are utilized; the basin of blood in both works is a visual symbol of the collusion and hypocrisy of all components of Spain's fascist regime. But in *And They Put Handcuffs on the Flowers,* Tosan's story is integrated into a broader dramatic framework. The tender scenes between Tosan and his wife, Falidia, clash with the horror of the relationship between another husband and wife which parallels that in *The Two Executioners.* Tosan's tragedy acquires additional meaning in this context, where the autobiographical element appears even more horrifying by contrast. The conclusion of *Hand-*

cuffs introduces a new element: when Tosan is garrotted, he demonstrates his human weakness by urinating out of fear as he expires. The women on stage catch the urine in a basin, dip their hands in it, and then wipe it on their faces. Miraculously, it has become blood; the basin of blood utilized earlier to indict the representatives of Spain's power structure becomes a symbol of hope.

The title is itself a striking poetic image, taken from the Spanish poet and playwright, Federico García Lorca, himself a victim of the Civil War. Lorca's death, described in the play in vivid detail, helps identify Arrabal's drama as a tragedy. One of the essential features of classical tragedy is the inevitability of the final disaster. In *Handcuffs* the incessant return to the reality of the prison cell and the irrevocability of Tosan's ultimate fate (underscored by the clock that ticks off the time remaining to him) confirm the tragic vision dominating the work. The figure of the Apparition, whose intermittent narration functions to describe the horrors of the Spanish penal system, augments the feeling of impending, ineluctable doom. The role playing within the dream sequences in which the same actors play both the suffering prisoners and their tormentors affirms the bond between all human beings while also communicating metaphorically, in a highly theatrical manner, man's inhumanity to man. In that abstract context, the tragedy transcends its Spanish setting and becomes truly universal.

Although Arrabal's plays have all had a strong visual component, *Handcuffs* develops that feature even further. Instead of utilizing slides and projections to heighten visuality, the playwright imbues his drama with a sensorial, cinematographic quality through the provocative use of stage movement and props. The bloodstained flag combines symbolically the colors white (innocence and purity) and red (blood and oppression) in a visual prop with thematic significance. By having a prisoner's wife (who represents Arrabal's mother) dance "The Dying Swan" while her husband is tortured, Arrabal depicts and protests political tyranny by means of a highly visual form of black humor.

The tone and aesthetic of *Handcuffs* is produced by the union of tenderness and pathos with the most violent form of blasphemy and grotesquerie yet employed by Arrabal. Some of these strident elements contribute positively to the impact of the staged play. But at times they become excessive and self indulgent, diminishing the efficacy of the socio-political statement. For the most part, those scenes and images which balance the horrorific and the repulsive with the comic, through invocation of the grotesque mode, serve good dramatic purposes. A prime example is the scene in which a sadistic priest is blinded and castrated. The horror of these acts is immediately tempered by the humor of the priest's scatological prayer, uttered reverently while he unctuously chews his own testicles.[10] Other blasphemies, however, such as the act of fellatio performed on the body of Christ, seem gratuitous and detract from the effect of the play.

Specific factual horrors of the Spanish Civil War are presented during the course of the drama. Several are obsessive motifs recurring in a number of subsequent works of different genres. These include the death of Lorca, killed by a shot in the rectum from the revolver òf a military officer offended by the poet's homosexuality, and the case of a man condemned to death for the murder of his town priest. When the latter presented himself to assure the tribunal that he had not been murdered by the accused, but instead had been saved by him, the sentence is changed to life imprisonment, since anyone able to save a priest must have had considerable influence among the Reds.

Autobiographical elements play a minor, but significant role. The play glorifies the memory of the author's father. In a role playing scene of great emotional impact for anyone acquainted with the salient facts of Arrabal's childhood, one prisoner assures another (the counterpart of Arrabal's father) that his children will learn the truth, that despite brainwashing, they will come to know and admire their imprisoned parent. By directly equating the prison cell with the womb, Arrabal reaffirms the idea of his own rebirth into socio-political awareness and rediscovery of the full psychological significance of his father.

And They Put Handcuffs on the Flowers is more successful as a theater performance than as a work of dramatic literature. Its structure, use of visual imagery, shock effects, grotesqueries, and the ability of the playwright to balance the extreme violence of some scenes with a pervasive lyrical quality combine to generate an exciting and moving theater experience. Nevertheless, the play suffers from an overall diffuseness, the sometimes gratuitous use of shock effects, and excesses related to audience participation. Arrabal has certainly not lost his ability to stir up controversy.[11] The dialectical quality which he has always sought to project on stage manifests itself here in the juxtaposition of scenes and images antithetical in nature, and in the ambiguity inherent in the play.

Throughout the drama, the prisoners allude to the first manned landing on the moon, an achievement seen as an absurd adventure in light of continued human suffering (prisons), although man's first peaceful conquest. The presence or absence of hope at the play's conclusion is elusively uncertain; Arrabal himself was unable to decide on a suitable ending.[12] The openness of the prisoners, their empathy toward one another, the love of Falidia and Tosan, and the affirmation that the children of a prisoner will discover the truth do provide a glimmer of hope based on the ineradicable nature of man's communal feelings. It is precisely this ambiguity, the uncertainty of man's salvation, juxtaposed with undeniable continuing abuses against the human spirit which provide *And They Put Handcuffs on the Flowers* a substantive base upon which to build and project a shout of protest.

III   Le Ciel et la Merde (Heaven and Shit)

Inspired by the Manson murders, *Heaven and Shit* (1970) employs audience participation,[13] the suppression of actor/spectator opposition, role playing by actors, and a loosely structured, episodic plot replaced near the end of the work by a specific event: the trial and execution of all of the characters. All of these features of the drama align it with *And They Put Handcuffs on the Flowers.* These two works share a number of motifs, but differ with respect to the perspective of the author. Arrabal was not directly involved with the Manson case, but saw in the event a subject through which he could examine and question basic premises of contemporary society. While exposing the *malaise* pervading our social structure, Arrabal, as is his wont, introduces the theme of eroticism. The mutual interdependence of love, religion, and societal norms emerges as the central focus of the entire work. The author's provocative use of scatology, sexual perversions, and blasphemy, in this critic's opinion, exceeds the boundaries dictated by the themes and tone of the play. However, *Heaven and Shit* does manage to disturb and stimulate its audience in a manner consonant with Arrabal's evolving preoccupation with socio-political institutions on an international scale.

Heaven and Shit utilizes stage action, props, music, and even odors to convert a theater performance into a religious ceremony. Three musicians play sacred music on oriental instruments throughout the work, while incense is burned. Before any characters appear, a rooster is heard crowing, introducing the motif of Christ, the savior, in the drama. Erasmus (Manson) comes forth; he is the prologue, and as such, introduces everyone involved in the production, which he refers to as a "religious meditation."[14] The other characters are Grouchenka, a slave in Czarist Russia, Cleaver, a former employee of a Boston insane asylum, and Judas and Ribla, a young couple. Ribla is pregnant and voices her desire to give birth to the messiah. All characters participate in enacting the horrors of the insane asylum, the master-slave relationship which structures their loves, an historico-fictitious scene between Christ returned to earth and the Grand Inquisitor of Seville, followed by the auction of Christ's body, and the joys of homosexual love. Their role playing, which structures the work to that point, is interrupted by a Voice announcing the trial of Erasmus and the others. The gruesome murders that they had committed are described in detail. The trial reaches a climax of orgiastic frenzy reminiscent of a musical bacchanale[15] in which the characters commit deviant sexual acts with one another while playing with the bloody remains of the people they had murdered. They are sentenced to death and mowed down by gunfire. Ribla's child emerges, and one of the musicians holds it aloft proclaiming the birth of the messiah.

A central component of *Heaven and Shit,* uniting the play's thematic content with its artistic vision, is insanity. The prominent role of the insane asylum identifies the institution as a metaphor representing all of society. Cleaver[16] is the character whose nightmarish experiences in the asylum become a focal point, but it is Erasmus' (Manson's insanity, implicit throughout, that is shown to be the logical result of his living in a mad society. Erasmus' sexual perversions, largely sadistic in nature, are mirrored by the physician in the asylum who punishes inmates by introducing spittle and urine into their bodies through a tube inserted in their nose (pp. 34-35).

The horror of the Manson killings, including the butchering of the pregnant Sharon Tate, has its counterpart in society's execution of the pregnant Ribla. Cleaver's loss of reason occurs when he unwittingly witnesses his parents' lovemaking; the hypocritical society in which he lives has allowed something natural and beautiful to become frightening and destructive. When the director of the asylum (symbolic of our society) finally realizes that Cleaver is not genuinely insane, he forces him to work with corpses, hoping to effect a mental breakdown so that Cleaver will conform to expectations of him. The motif of insanity contributes to the oneiric, frenzied quality of the drama; and the schizophrenic nature of our society is underscored by the numerous antinomies connoted by the title.

Heaven and Shit is a theatrical ceremony closely aligned with religious ritual, as evidenced by the central role accorded the concept of messiah. Charles Manson, of course, was a self proclaimed messiah. The violence and cruelty in the play can be related to the horror of Christ's crucifixion. In order to ascend to heaven, Jesus had to suffer cruelties and indignities emanating from man's moral corruption; these are alluded to in the title of the play ("shit"). Before announcing that she is pregnant with the messiah, Ribla first blesses the telephone, the refrigerator, and other such products of technology. In a society which worships these items, the messiah will be "little like a flea, ugly like a roach and golden like a beetle" (p. 30). Materialism corrupts; by having Judas take the role of Christ, Arrabal depicts man selling himself out, capitulating to his own perverse instincts, fostered by the society in which he lives, wherein goodness and naturalness become a threat. That was the case in Spain during the Golden Age; thus the Grand Inquisitor sentences Christ to death because he is dangerous to the church. The true spirit of Jesus could not survive in the past, and is even more of an anathema now. In the perverse world of inverted values, the new Venus de Milo will be a slobbering toad, and the messiah will be conceived from the sodomy of two homosexuals and will eat excrement and drink urine. On one level, Erasmus is a grotesque deformation of Christ, but he does show an affinity for love (albeit sadistic) and nature that seems almost admirable in light of society's hypocrisies. Ribla's child, a girl resembling the insects she said it would, had been born out of murder and violence. She is a messiah, however, incorporating hope for salvation (the "heaven" of the title), a new generation that may yet dismiss the false ideology propagated in today's world.

Ribla's essentially masochistic erotic visions are compared to the mystical hallucinations of Saint Theresa and the fantasies of the Marquis de Sade (two personages who, for Arrabal, are one and the same individual). As in numerous other works, Arrabal attacks Spanish Catholicism for fostering a sado-masochistic view of love.[17] In *Heaven and Shit,* religion and sexuality are closely aligned; the freedom man's savior will bring will encompass love making as well. Erasmus' presentation of God as love or orgasm (p. 36) makes the identification between spiritual and sexual freedom explicitly clear. Scatology, torture, sodomy and fellatio are practiced with an energy ultimately cathartic. In seeking to prepare the way for the liberation of mankind, *Heaven and Shit,* like *Ars Amandi* and *Erotic Bestiality,* suggests that human tenderness and love can be only achieved by first experiencing and then transcending lust, depravity and filth.

As in many of Arrabal's dramas, the central aesthetic of *Heaven and Shit* reflects its principal theme. The grotesque figures prominently, dominating the view of love and religion. As in *And They Put Handcuffs on the Flowers,* grotesque scenes remain highly cinematographic in quality. One example, which has a counterpart in both *Handcuffs* and the film *Viva la muerte (Long Live Death),* is the scene where actresses in the drama sing "I Love Paris" and dance gaily around Cleaver as he is force fed urine and spittle through a tube. The final orgy preceding the execution of all of the characters would be best realized in the medium of film. The central dialectic of the grotesque mode announced in the title unites humor with blasphemy and pornography to produce the play's most striking images which function to undermine established societal values.[18]

Heaven and Shit is a disturbing play. Its excesses are so extreme that it becomes difficult to defend the work against a charge of sensationalism.[19] The event which inspired it was so totally depraved that its literary exploitation must be questioned. However, despite loose structure and elements of gratuitous horror, *Heaven and Shit* raises significant questions about the values of contemporary society. The play closely resembles *Handcuffs* both in style and dramatic technique. But its characters, culled from today's counterculture, are reminiscent of the childlike beings dominant in Arrabal's earliest plays. Their amorality, as in the works of the 1950s, stands in direct opposition to the hypocritical norms of society. Like the early dramas, *Heaven and Shit* also affirms the link between theater and religious ceremony. Just as Christ's sacrifice has become the basis for the ritual of the Mass, Manson's messianic deed is now the ritual entitled *Heaven and Shit.* The birth of Ribla's child perpetuates the cyclic search for a savior to deliver man from society's excremental vision and show him a path to pure, honest love.

IV   La grande revue du XXe siècle
(The Great Revue of the Twentieth Century)

The Great Revue of the Twentieth Century (1970) further develops Arrabal's critique of the corruption and hypocrisy rampant in
our contemporary technological society. The vantage point from
which the dramatist presents these twentieth-century satirical
sketches is again modern counterculture. In *The Great Revue of the
Twentieth Century* the perspective is intensified even more. Marie
Satanas, the central character through whom all of the skits are
presented, smokes marijuana before each. The atmosphere of the
drama unique in Arrabal's theater, combines the dream-like, dis-
orienting feeling of a drug induced hallucination with the gaiety of
a music hall revue. Once again a clash between content and form
intensifies the dramatic tension.

The Great Revue of the Twentieth Century consists of a prologue
and six independent sketches. Marie Satanas belongs to a family
living close to nature, having rejected all of modern technology.
When a man driving a car penetrates their secluded domain, the
family tears him apart. Inside his vehicle, Marie, a thirteen year old
girl, finds a book entitled *Le XXe siècle raconté par l'image (The
Twentieth Century Through Pictures)*. While smoking marijuana
given to her by her father, she begins to read the book. The content
of the volume is transformed into hallucinatory musical sketches in
which Marie takes a role.

The first sketch, "Hiroshima and Einstein," depicts the horror
of the A-bomb attack on Hiroshima, the satanic glee of a caricature
of Truman, and the remorse of Einstein over the product of his
theory of relativity. The next skit, "The Olympic Games and
Landru," is a spoof of the whole concept of the Olympics (and our
competitive society) in which there are events for prostitutes, cripples, perverts, epileptics, and more. This satiric view of athletic
contests is combined with the execution of Landru, the mad
assassin who cooked a dozen women in his oven. Marie, his last victim, emerges from the oven to win the marathon and light the
Olympic flame. Unfortunately, the entire stadium goes up in
flames; three black athletes emerge from the holocaust to make the
sign of black power.

"Hitler in his Bunker" presents the dictator as a weak old man
with nervous tics who, as the symbol of the Aryan race, is conscious of the irony in his confession to his fiancée Eva Braun that

he has only one testicle. That admission becomes the refrain of a satirical ditty followed by Hitler's suicide. "The Virgin of Fatima and the Flying Saucers" juxtaposes an extraterrestrial warning of doom through atomic destruction with the hypocritical commercialization and exploitation of a religious miracle. "The Tragedy of the Titanic, Freud and the Sexual Revolution" interweaves the disaster of the sinking of the Titanic, Freud's theories, their reception — and a contemporary "happening." The final sketch, "The Crimes and the Moon," juxtaposes the first manned landing on the moon with the horror of a long series of recent political murders and assassinations.[20] A final song, addressed to the audience, concludes the work.

The Great Revue of the Twentieth Century has more structure than its title and format suggest. The pursuit by the police of Marie Satanas for her role in the murder of the man in the car lends a semblance of linear plot. And the presence of Marie in each of the episodes provides a central focus. Her surname which means "devil" in Spanish, complements the satanic frenzy gradually subsuming the atmosphere of the drama, and equating twentieth-century society with the horrors of hell. Although a "revue," the play's themes, motifs and stylistic devices maintain the continuity between its seemingly distinct sketches. The nuclear destruction depicted in the first skit is reinforced by the spaceman's warning of impending doom on earth in the fourth section. Society's supercilious rejection of the warning is mirrored in the attitude of the passengers on the Titanic in the following episode. Marie Satanas' drug induced hallucinations become more and more frightening; both she and the audience are plunged into a nightmare resulting from the frenetic vision of man refusing to save his fellow human beings on the sinking Titanic. The nightmare intensifies, climaxing in the projection of the assassinations of leading personalities of the century, each visual image accompanied by a piercing scream. The climax of the entire play, the arrest of Marie, becomes supremely ironic in light of the arresting officer's preceding comment to her. "At least you will be leaving the world of insanity where you live," he says. "You are going toward civilization."[21]

The Great Revue of the Twentieth Century is perhaps Arrabal's wittiest drama. Bettina Knapp, in her review of the work, observes that Arrabal has reached new heights of satiric verve in the play.[22] This is evident in the songs, particularly those dealing with the Olympic games.[23] The songs, the projections, the episodic structure of the drama, and the concluding lyrics addressed directly to the audience, all suggest that Arrabal has sought inspiration for this didactic play from the theater of Bertold Brecht. Succinctly summarizing the essential qualities of Brechtian epic theater, Harold Clurman helps identify *The Great Revue of the Twentieth Century* as an avant-garde Brechtian work by stating: "Brecht's plays are picaresque, poetic narrations for the stage. They are based on brief episodes of concentrated action — most of them complete in themselves — each of which makes a simple sharp point essential to the understanding of the play's idea as a whole. The intellectual approach is tersely factual, the tone ironic, crisp and detached. Songs in a similar vein embody the ideological point as in an epigram."[24] Arrabal's use of historical figures contrasts with Brecht's fondness for exotic settings and parables; his penchant for the nightmarish vision also distinguishes his work from Brechtian theater. In most of his dramas, Arrabal's aesthetic and technique are substantially different from Brecht's. But in this didactic, political play, his themes and dramatic methodology have a great deal in common with those of the German dramatist Brecht. Ideologically, they share what Robert Brustein perceives to be the *Weltanschauung* of Brecht, who is "torn between the purity of the ideal and the mud of earthly reality, between a vision of the changing tomorrow and a vision of the unchanging today."[25]

Arrabal, in *The Great Revue of the Twentieth Century,* has sacrificed the magnetic quality of his earlier theater that resulted from the audience's direct contact with a creative, anguished psyche (the author's). But his drama has gained in humor and topicality. He no longer immerses spectators in a highly original dramatic milieu, at once disorienting, demonic, and poetic. Yet the essential clash between form and content, the ability to create an alluring, nonrealistic ambience, the satanic wit and the remarkable diversity of theatrical technique have continued to develop. The result, if less moving than some of Arrabal's better pre-1970 plays, is still provocative and entrancing.

V   La Guerre de mille ans (The Thousand Year War)

Written in the same vein as *The Great Revue of the Twentieth Century, The Thousand Year War* (1971-1972) also utilizes songs and dramatic sketches or tableaux to attack capitalist society, its colonialism, hypocrisy and repressions. The published text contains several variations of scenes and additional songs and scenes as well; for reasons of expediency, only the integral version of the play will be considered in this analysis. *The Thousand Year War,* unlike Arrabal's other plays, was not inspired by the author's subjective vision but rather is the product of the dramatist's political discussions with friends, collective efforts in which Arrabal sought to translate into dramatic images ideas expressed in conversation.[26] Although reflecting the author's wit and satiric verve by using music, sound, light and stage images in a manner closely associated with Arrabal, the work fails to project a coherent dramatic vision. It is an attempt at musical theater lacking the hallucinatory quality and Brechtian style of Arrabal's previous play, offering little in their stead. Explicit Marxist doctrine, didactic sermonizing and lack of incisiveness cause the piece to appear more like a political statement than a work of dramatic art.

The Thousand Year War consists of three scenes or tableaux, the setting for the first suggesting a concentration camp. The play's themes are military discipline, education as brainwashing, culture controlled by money and the state, and the masses mesmerized and deluded by the media. These ideas are communicated through songs and skits utilizing allegorical figures representing culture, the press, the writer, television and others. The central vision of this first scene can best be described as excremental; in one exemplifying episode, the Nobel Prize winning writer wipes Capital's anus with toilet paper which he then uses to produce another book, the best selling, *Memories of the Master.* The second scene consists of a rugby match, sponsored by Coca-Cola (Capitalism), between conservatives of the new world and the traditionalists of the Christian west. Its climax is a scathing denunciation of imperialism in which a poor native is eviscerated and devoured by the leader of a colonializing army. Justice, allegorized as a bare breasted female, is shown to be conveniently blind, while religion (the Pope) sanctimoniously applauds the army's destruction of the revolutionaries. The final scene simulates a bullfight. The animal, a symbol of the revolution, is brutally tortured and slain. Its eyes are then auctioned off to the highest bidder who gleefully devours them. Arrabal's mordant humor is exercised with particular aplomb in the scene in which a number of other items are sold, including an underdeveloped country whose population is ninety-eight percent illiterate which "comes" with a guarantee that no Marxist leaders reside there. The repressions of the established regime are carried out from the airplane which is the seat of the government; but the President's enumeration of dangerous elements in society is soon replaced by the revolutionary song, "Bella Ciao" ("Beautiful Farewell")[27] which constitutes an apotheosis affirming the glory of dying for freedom.

The Thousand Year War has elements of biting satire and acerbic wit. But in his enthusiasm for the play's message, Arrabal has failed to construct a unified dramatic work with its own reality in the theater. Essentially propaganda, its humorous moments are clever and its memorable images shocking. However, they fail to mesh in a manner touching the human spirit of the audience. As one reviewer commented, "what is notable is only that the shock which Arrabal has been so diligently preparing doesn't quite last long enough."[28] It may be that the dramatist's call for revolution, inspired by political discussions and camaraderie, lacks the passion or structure resulting from Arrabal's normal method of writing, where images and form spring directly from his own mind and soul. In any case, *The Thousand Year War* emphasizes politics over art, humor and sarcasm more than imagination and dramatic synthesis. In his political zeal, Arrabal has sacrificed his dramatic talent for the sake of didacticism.

VI   La marcha real (The Royal March)

Written in 1973 for Jérôme Savary's "Magic Circus,"[29] *The Royal March* is a brief, vitriolic farce dealing with Franco and his successor, Prince Juan Carlos. The central vision is reminiscent of Valle-Inclán's *esperpentos* in its dependence upon caricature, deformation, and the grotesque. Satiric songs figure prominently in the mockery of leaders of the Spanish government.

The first scene presents Franco hunting; his servants help to maintain pretenses by telling their leader that he has killed forty-eight birds with only sixteen shots — when in fact he has not really shot anything. (They have a supply of dead animals to bring back to him.) After the sarcastic song of the hunters reminds the audience of all of the blood on Franco's hands, the dictator appears to express concern to his wife that his system may not continue after his death. She warns him against the exiled king, Don Juan, with his liberal ideas.

In the following scene, Don Juan forces his son, Juan Carlos, to swear, on all fours, that he will never betray his father and accept the throne. The young prince thereafter quickly reveals his true nature by treacherously killing his brother, Alfonso. Franco is so impressed with him as a result of the nefarious act that he summons him to court to induce him to remain and study. With the aid of the leader of the Military, Franco succeeds in brainwashing the Prince; at a session of the Spanish Parliament, Juan Carlos is named heir to the throne in a grotesque coronation ceremony. The situation is complicated by the marriage of Franco's granddaughter to Juan Carlos' cousin, Alfonso. Franco is intrigued by the idea of his great-grandchildren occupying the throne. Juan Carlos and Alfonso exchange insults and decide to fight a duel; their mutual cowardice causes them to eschew traditional weapons and make it a contest of flatulence. At the play's conclusion, the hymn of the Spanish Republic is heard and the Spanish people sweep Franco and the entire royal family away, raising the fists in triumph.

The Royal March is a minor work, reasonably effective because of its appropriate brevity and incisive wit. One example of the latter occurs in the initial hunting scene when Franco, referring to the pheasants he has been shooting, asks how many he has killed. His chief military officer responds, "millions." Franco then clarifies his question in the following manner: "I'm not speaking of Spaniards, I'm speaking of birds."[30] Arrabal's penchant for black humor reaches its zenith in the coronation scene where Juan Carlos enters with a pig and is crowned by Franco while on his hands and knees so that the Spanish dictator can sodomize the new heir to the throne at the climax of the ceremony. Juan Carlos then shouts: "Yupiii! Now I'm king. My Oedipus complex is over and done with" (p. 23). Franco, deeply moved by the Prince's declaration, cries and has a spasm.

The principal aesthetic of *The Royal March* is the grotesque. Arrabal's vision of the royal family is especially evident in his portrayal of Jaime, the true heir to the throne, as a mute epileptic. *The Royal March* seeks to shock and offend in order to protest what the dramatist perceives to be the perverse nature of the Spanish ruler and his chosen successor. The drama is simplistic, and its scope certainly quite narrow; but within those limitations, it achieves the author's intent.

VII   Sur le Fil ou La Ballade du train fantôme
(On the Wire or The Ballad of the Phantom Train)

On the Wire was directly inspired by a chance event which had a profound emotional effect on its author. While traveling in New Mexico in April, 1974, Arrabal noticed a roadsign for the town of Madrid. His curiosity caused him to abandon his itinerary and investigate this unexpected reminder of his native country in the desert of the southwestern United States. He soon discovered that Madrid, New Mexico, was a ghost town; it had once been a thriving community with a championship baseball team but the closing of its sole industry, a coal mine, resulted in an abrupt mass exodus. Intrigued by the metaphoric possibilities of this other Madrid, Arrabal converted his intense personal feelings about his own exile into his most original drama of the 1970s.

The action of *On the Wire* occurs near the entrance to a mine in the ghost town of Madrid, New Mexico. Tharsis, the exiled Spaniard (Arrabal's counterpart), arrives the duke of Gaza, a young Spanish nobleman whom he has kidnapped at the latter's suggestion. Their suitcase contains a telephone they use to communicate with the Duke's father in Madrid, Spain. Upon arriving in Madrid, New Mexico, Tharsis is overcome with nostalgia for Spain; he performs a traditional dance of his country and then collapses weeping. The sound of applause serves to introduce Wichita, the third character in the play. A tight-rope walker, he is the only remaining inhabitant of the ghost town. In a dialogue among the three men, their feelings about each of the Madrids are expressed. Wichita is unable to perform his circus act successfully for the others, but does communicate to Tharsis the full significance of his art. Tharsis swears to cross the Puerta del Sol in Madrid (Spain) on a high wire in order to affirm the freedom of all Spaniards in art and life.

Throughout the play the sound of a roaring train is heard periodically. It appears to be descending into the mine in order to remove the skeletons of men and horses. But nobody can be seen actually operating the train. Wichita cryptically requests that his body be placed in the mine when he dies so that it may also be picked up by the phantom train. In a brief ritual, Wichita bids farewell to his companions and to the birds he magically commands, transfers his "art" to Tharsis by kissing the latter's feet, and then plunges into the well descending into the mine to his death. The Duke, using binoculars, discovers the truth about the phantom train but refuses to disclose it to Tharsis, insisting that it is too horrible to tell.

In the play's final scene, the two surviving characters are in the Puerta del Sol in Madrid, Spain. Before beginning his climactic stunt, Tharsis demands to know the secret of the phantom train. The Duke finally explains that the train belongs to a dog food company which uses the corpses of men and horses (with their flesh miraculously preserved) to produce their product. Tharsis begins his act; the Spanish government sends a helicopter to shoot him down but the intervention of Wichita's birds protects Tharsis. He begins to do more and more difficult feats on the wire to the accompaniment of the people's shouts for liberty and the singing of a Hallelujah.

The play's two titles, *On the Wire* and *The Ballad of the Phantom Train,* allude to the dichotomy of imagery and theme providing much of the dramatic tension. The train, in conjuction with the mine, comes to represent death. It is a metaphor for the decadence and sterility of a Spain crippled by political oppression. The full import of the horror perpetrated by that government is revealed in the shocking image of human beings debased to the extent that they become food for animals. The symbol of the wire stands in opposition to the train; it comes to represent the heights to which the human soul can and must aspire through the liberating power of the arts. In order to reach those heights, the artist must first seek his inspiration in the depths of human grime, sweat and pain.[31] Like Malik in *A Tortoise Named Dostoievsky,* the miners have magical visions while inside the earth. Wichita describes the sensations he experienced while surrounded by water, coal, dust and mud; a delicate, white virgin had embraced him, he said, and asked him to give her a child.[32] Dualities abound in *On the Wire.* They are reflected in the changing relationships between characters; however, the primary source of dialectical tension is the existence of the two separate Madrids. Each elucidates the nature and situation of the other in a kaleidoscope of changing reflections. Spain's capital emerges ultimately as the unified focus of the play, its malaise having been underscored in counterpoint by the town of the same name in New Mexico.[33]

On the thematic level, the dialectical imagery that structures the entire play unites the political with the personal. Arrabal's identification with Tharsis is patently clear; the words of the character often express the concerns and the anguish of their exiled author: "It is forbidden to speak of me, it is forbidden to present what I do; one may only mention me if it is to slander or to injure me. They have just written that I should be castrated in order to prevent me from producing any children who might be like me" (p. 80).

Like Arrabal, the character Tharsis had left Spain because he could not breathe there;[34] again, this idea resonates with its counterpart in the other Madrid where the miners succumb to black lung disease. Tharsis (Arrabal) speaks of the horrors of his religious upbringing in post-Civil War Spain; these contrast with Wichita's ecstatic memories of his descent into the mine. Tharsis identifies with Spain's other illustrious exiles (Picasso and Casals, among others), but the Duke confronts him with the painful truth. Those artists — like Tharsis — became the "anti-Spain" during their lives, only to be acclaimed and acknowledged in their country after their death. Such is the exiled Tharsis' fate: his only hope for recognition lying in death, while those who remain can claim, *if* things change, that *they stayed* to fight against repression, unlike the exiles who chose the easy solution.[35]

Arrabal's personal anguish with respect to his feelings about exile provides a dramatic intensity lacking in several of his endeavors immediately preceding *On the Wire*. But the success of the play cannot and does not depend exclusively on its direct autobiographical component. By interweaving these concerns with an artistic vision based on several striking metaphors, Arrabal integrates his principal theme, artistic endeavor, within the context of a highly original and visually compelling dramatic milieu.

On the Wire is an important play precisely because it transcends personal and political concerns. Creative art, as symbolized by tight-rope walking, is an abstract and highly personal skill which cannot be taught. It liberates the artist by incorporating death into a life giving, inspiring act. Tharsis envisions his performance as follows: "Alone, like the artist, defying the danger and the threat and embracing death... I shall be infinitely alone and infinitely free on top of a wire that will be mine and that belongs to me from the beginning of my life. I would like to be the poet in the air" (p. 99). Wichita, Tharsis' artistic mentor, recalls the Architect, in *The Architect and the Emperor of Assyria,* because of his power over the birds. The transference of Wichita's artistic powers has a ritualistic quality recalling the earlier scene in which the Architect devours the Emperor and assimilates his essence. It is Wichita's suicide that relegates his corporal being to the dogs; the act is necessary to effect the transfer of his artistic spirit to Tharsis allowing the latter's climactic feat in his native Spain to take place. Art is aligned with passion, hatred, and death. Wichita counsels Tharsis: "And don't forget: hate as you hate now ... only in that way will you succeed in being a great poet of the high wire" (p. 103).

The final creative act over Madrid's Puerta del Sol unites these conflicting elements into a climactic affirmation of the power of art to liberate man, both spiritually and politically. The equation of the mine with the womb is extended by Tharsis' statement from above the Puerta del Sol affirming the rebirth of man through art by linking the wire to the birth process. He remarks: "The wire is my umbilical cord. It is like a tape that emerges from my belly, and coils around the wire, forming it" (p. 115). The depths (the mine) of human existence have become the source and inspiration for man's noblest acts. The union of opposites, the key to Panic art, is affirmed by Tharsis' description of the "temptation of falling" as a sexual drive resulting from his androgynous feelings on the wire (p. 115). In Freudian terms, a train trip symbolizes death. But here, the train's penetration of the mine also suggests the life giving sexual act. *On the Wire* elevates life's dualities and antinomies to the level of myth, capturing the magnitude of the act of artistic creation.

On the Wire combines the intensely personal feelings of the dramatist, political realities, and dramatic metaphors into a unified, coherent treatment of the role of art in the modern world, and allows Arrabal to exorcize what has become a central dilemma in his own life, "the deracination and dehumanization that comes with exile."[36] The play confirms that the playwright's talent lies in his ability to convert personal concerns into dramatic images at once haunting, poetic, provocative and disturbing. Without abandoning the political awareness which characterizes his dramas of the 1970s, Arrabal has returned to his strengths as a writer and produced a didactic work comparing favorably with his finest previous plays in aesthetic value, theatrical technique, and humanistic significance.

VIII   Les jeunes barbares d'aujourd'hui
(Today's Young Barbarians)

Today's Young Barbarians, written in 1975, unites Arrabal's Marxist view of class struggle with features of style and atmosphere associated with his early theater. Most names as well as the central vision of the work derive directly from Lewis Carroll. Kafka's Theater of Oklahoma and concept of metamorphosis also give direction to the piece. There is a strong erotic component psychologically justifiable by the dream-like atmosphere. The concept of theater is closely aligned with ceremony; the Eucharist becomes a central ritual uniting the fantasy world of *Alice in Wonderland* to the motif of the bicycle race. During the climactic competition, several racers whose names are taken from Carroll's works are identified as the "young barbarians" who will lead the revolt, through art, against the oppressions of the privileged class. Arrabal has returned to his original sources of artistic inspiration seeking a propitious medium for expressing his social concerns.

Today's Young Barbarians begins on a Pirandellian note. Eçila's introductory song is interrupted by the chance arrival of three characters — Dumpty, Chester and Tenniel[37] — who voice conjectures about what lies behind the as yet unraised curtain. Chester then addresses the audience; his words, "The Great Theater of Oklahoma calls you for the first and the last time,"[38] precede the play proper. Chester and Tenniel are bicycle racers while Dumpty, who is blind, serves as their masseur. They live in poverty under the domination of Snarck, whose luxurious lifestyle is maintained at their expense. They detest this malevolent character who never appears but, when he calls them on the telephone, treat him with servility. Chester becomes the first character to introduce what will be a long series of allusions to *Alice in Wonderland*. He discovers the names Tweedledee and Tweedledum written in the theater, and tells the others about his encounter with the white rabbit. The sexually naive Kitty enters and joins Chester and Tenniel in a nightmarish caricature of the mad tea party episode from *Alice in Wonderland* in which they all stuff huge amounts of jam and bread into their mouths and into the sleeping Dumpty's.

When Dumpty awakens, he explains how he had lost his sight in a bicycle race by falling off a wall. He now works for Snarck, dispensing the same drugs to Tenniel and Chester he himself had been obliged to take before his accident. Kitty drinks a bottle of liquid she has found and shrinks, like Alice, so that she is able to view a miniature bicycle race through a tiny door. Christ, who bears a striking resemblance to Chester, overtakes Dracula and leads the race. Eçila then announces that the "big" race will begin in twenty minutes. She brings a flask of blood which Dumpty had purportedly extracted from Snarck while the latter was sleeping, in order to weaken him. Dumpty returns to utilize the blood in conferring communion on Chester, Eçila and Kitty.

As the climactic race begins, Tenniel declares himself and Chester "today's young barbarians." He and Chester are soon far in front of the other racers, as Snarck falls farther and farther behind. But suddenly Chester gets off his bike with the finish line in sight[39] and announces he is going to join the white rabbit. He then metamorphoses into Don Quixote,[40] falls off a precipice, becomes blind, and ecstatically sees the glory and the beauty of God's world. The other characters join him; they all hold candles which provide the only illumination in the theater. The candles are then extinguished and the play concludes in total darkness.

The two central metaphors structuring *Today's Young Barbarians* equate life with theater and with a bicycle race. The magical ambience of that theater derives from Lewis Carroll's fantasy world; its ethereal nature is articulated by Chester while he searches for the stage lights. He comments, "I am looking for the light, but I am not finding anything; this must be a theater of Chinese shadows for invisible Martian hares or for black birds of memory."[41] This magical quality inherent in Arrabalian theater has the power of transforming reality, as Dumpty's statement indicates: "The theater, that must be dancing eternally on oneself, turning like a magician until you levitate and fly through the air" (p. 21). Tenniel, in his anguish over his subservient status, speaks of the theater of life in which he and his friends are denied the right to play even the smallest role (p. 22). However, this theater within a theater which is the social reality for the masses of today's world is transformed by the theatrical ritual in which Snarck's blood is used by Dumpty to bestow communion on the others. By constructing varying levels of theater, Arrabal depicts man's situation and the solution to it through a single unifying metaphor.

The bicycle race, providing intensity and energy derived from the author's passion for that sport, also becomes a metaphor for the competitive nature of society reflected in class structure. The use of an athletic contest to symbolize a socio-economic condition has an antecedent in Arrabal's theater; the rugby match in *The Thousand Year War* played a similar role.[42] Dumpty's justification to Eçila of drugs to stimulate the cyclists integrates the motifs of theater, sports and the class struggle in a single statement:

In a bicycle race, all of the miseries and all of the exaltations of life intersect amidst the noise and the furor: it is a love story featuring depraved beings who feel the bee's blood and grow excited under the sting of the command and of the humiliation; it is a monarchy with kings who mastur-

bate in the midst of resentments, of complots and of wreaths of flowers; it
is a factory where one witnesses the struggle between classes, it is a war
with soldiers who fight and chocolate generals who monopolize the
honors; it is the great theater of the world with dusty actors and actresses
whom the public applauds and of stage hands who do not appear under
any arch of triumph (pp. 29–30).

In dreaming of victory, Tenniel affirms the need for revolt:
"Without thinking for a single minute of aiding Snarck, we will
revolt: the servants, the herd against the privileged class, the poor
against those who possess everything ... we will be today's young
barbarians" (p. 41). But the real triumph belongs to Chester. By
following the white rabbit, a symbol of the artistic vision of Lewis
Carroll (which, in turn, has been assimilated by Arrabal), Chester
rejects the concept of competition. The miniscule bicycles he
extracts from his pockets to confirm that he is already a champion
allude to the previous race in miniature where he appeared as
Christ. Chester's metamorphosis into Don Quixote is both a sacrifice and a triumph; by negating the values of the material world, he
transcends them. By plunging over a precipice and losing his sight,
Chester experiences a higher form of vision which in its reference to
God and the creation of the world also evokes the conceit, "all the
world's a stage," and alludes obliquely to the Great Theater of
Oklahoma. Chester has heeded the call of this theater, confirming
Arrabal's artistic vision derived from Carroll and Kafka as a propitious means of both attacking and transcending man's subjugation
of his fellow man.

Today's Young Barbarians represents an attempt by its author to
return to the sources of artistic inspiration which had served him
well in the past and to use them to address current concerns. The
magical quality of the play's atmosphere may not seem entirely
suitable to his didactic purpose. But even Lewis Carroll's delightful
fantasies have a serious and, at times, sinister dimension. Arrabal's
affirmation of the power of art becomes as strong a theme as his
denunciation of social injustice. *Today's Young Barbarians* is an
effective piece of dramatic literature because it succeeds in linking
disparate motifs and themes into a unified artistic vision well served
by the author's return to the sources and techniques having proved
productive for him throughout his career.

IX   La Gloire en Images (Glory in Images)

In an interview published by Mel Gussow in *The New York*

Times in 1972,[43] Arrabal stated that his next play would deal with
Gilles de Rais, the fifteenth-century French marshall executed for
sexually assaulting and murdering thousands of children. Arrabal
was intrigued by this character who had some of the qualities of
Jekyl and Hyde because, despite his heinous crimes, he was a gen-
erous man who donated his entire fortune to charity. Arrabal
promised in the interview that the drama he would write would not
be merely an historical work, but would relate directly to our
contemporary world. *Glory in Images* was not published or performed until four years after the interview. Its initial production
was exceedingly lavish, featuring a large orchestra and corps de
ballet. It was staged in German translation at the Bremen Opera
House.

Glory in Images is a ballet which alternates dance, movement,
and improvised speech, all carefully described by the author, with
the text, in verse, to be chanted or sung by some of the characters.
The plot is an essentially chronological presentation of the life of
Gilles de Rais, from birth to execution. The use of the art form,
ballet, provides a visual component underscoring the dream-like
atmosphere. The strange yet recognizable armor of the soldiers
who dance at the beginning of the piece immediately establishes the
nightmarish vision. Visual images, energized by movement and
music, unite themes and aesthetics into a coherent whole.

As in many of Arrabal's finest works, a series of antinomies provides the play with its dramatic tension. This dialectical quality is
introduced visually in the opening scene in the form of White and
Black, dancing abstractions who crystallize into Gilles de Rais and
Joan of Arc.[44] The dual nature of Gilles himself is concretized by
the character's inverse — or conscience — Rais le Hérault. The
latter emerges from inside a grotesquely swollen Gilles de Rais in a
parody of the sublimity and violence of his own birth. They dance
together, clinging to one another in a supremely human and erotic
manner confirming their metaphysical inseparability. Three grotesque puppets — Bishop Cauchon, the Duke of Brittany, and the
monarch Charles VII — sing of Gilles' birth into a troubled
society. Addressing Gilles, the Bishop employs an image which
underscores the protagonists's dual nature: "You carry the veil of
the virginal bride with the sword that shines between your
thighs."[45] This fundamental duality, which here takes the form of
an androgyne, is developed throughout the work in Gilles' penchant for alchemy, his constant struggle with the pure element in

himself (Rais le Hérault), and his affinities with Christ and Don Quixote which clash with his own diabolical nature and depraved crimes.

In *Glory in Images* Arrabal utilizes all of the arts to infuse his subject with a provocative, dazzling sensuality which virtually assaults the spectator. The plastic arts figure prominently throughout — Goya and his black paintings are directly evoked. The Sorceress-Whore who dances in the fourth episode, enveloped in a black cape, is a central component of the allusion to Goya. She paints a dead child (Gilles' victim) black, and then summons the devil in the form of a goat.[46] The principal dichotomy is expanded in the fifth episode as the Sorceress and Gilles (the forces of evil) form a *"pas de quatre"* with Joan of Arc and Rais le Hérault (purity). The black mass then conducted, featuring sensual music and swirling dancers, suggests the *Walpurgisnacht* of Charles Gounod's *Faust*, an opera of which Arrabal is especially fond.[47] The grotesque carnival scene of the sixth and penultimate episode is explicitly linked to Goya's painting "The Burial of the Sardine."

Arrabal's virtuoso exercise in aesthetics in *Glory in Images* should not cause the spectator to lose sight of its personal and socio-political components. Societal institutions are caricatured in the grotesque puppets[48] representing the Duke, the Bishop and the King who sentence both Gilles de Rais and Joan of Arc to death in parallel scenes exposing their hypocrisy. Gilles' extravagant crimes constitute only one aspect of his being. He insists that in excrement and perversion he sought the final step to apotheosis, that he hoped to find in the center of infamy and evil God's voice affirming His love for him (p. 116). Gilles' affirmation of love, even in pain and torture, his fascination with alchemy, and the idea that to reach heaven one must first pass through an earthly hell, all mirror Arrabal's own creed in theater. *Glory in Images*, on one level, may well be a metaphor representing all of the dramatist's theater. As such, it reminds the spectator that scatology, pornography, and the grotesque, central features of this work and much of Arrabal's drama, should not cause the poetic, sentimental, and profoundly human elements — the real substance of the author's artistic vision — to be overlooked. The real "glory" of his theater is its "images" — musical, visual and linguistic — which unite into a dazzling whole thematic concerns and aesthetic techniques.

X   La Tour de Babel (The Tower of Babel)

Arrabal's last published work, *The Tower of Babel,* is dated March 13, 1976. In a manner similar to *On the Wire,* the play presents the author's feelings about his native country and his exile from it. Both plays achieve much of their dramatic impact through use of several highly original and provocative central symbols. *The Tower of Babel* exposes the soul of Spain in a panoramic vision encompassing past and present and blending the real and the ideal, farce, melodrama and satire. In the broadest sense, the play constitutes an analysis of its author's psyche and artistic technique within the context of his feelings toward his own native land.

The action of *The Tower of Babel* transpires in Villa Ramiro, the fictitious name Arrabal uses for Ciudad Rodrigo in Spain. The dialectical quality, a frequent component of the author's dramatic vision, is immediately introduced in the stage directions by two central symbols: the termites which eventually destroy the castle from within and the eagles soaring majestically above the structure. Latidia, the blind Duchess of Teran,[49] rules over the castle; she lives in the past, immersed in dreams and memories evoking the glories of Spain's history. She dotes on the ass from Mars[50] now residing in the moat surrounding the castle. Latidia refuses to abandon the castle — which has been sold as a result of her bankruptcy to the Count and Countess d'Ecija. Her impassioned plea for assistance in defending it echoes the words of La Pasionaria[51] — the Duchess alludes to the Spanish Civil War and to great battles of Spanish history, swearing never to surrender the castle.

As a response to her call, volunteers begin to arrive for the "International Brigade." The hired killer and the three beggars who come represent a grotesque caricature of the volunteers during the Spanish Civil War. The Count and Countess, served by the Marquis de Cerralbo, decide to humor Latidia by allowing her to believe she is still in control in order to avoid an international scandal.[52] Latidia assigns an identity to each of the other characters; her servant Mareda becomes Teresa of Ávila, the Count and Countess are Goya and Doña Jimena, the three beggars are Don Juan, El Cid and Che Guevara, and so on. These characters eventually come to identify with their assigned roles. In the interim, the beggars take control of the castle, torturing and abusing the "nobility" in a grotesque banquet scene reminiscent of the one in Luis Buñuel's film *Viridiana.* Pornography in the form of sadomasochism, bondage and love slavery (in the style of Pauline Reàge's *The Story of O*) dominate the central scenes. In the eleventh scene, the Martian Ass becomes a man; and Latidia, in a typical Arrabalian reversal, begins to bray. The ass is dressed as a bride (the androgyne) and speaks like a person. Latidia and the Martian, now à pilgrim, descend ladders together in search of the lost plans for the Tower of Babel. Every rung of the ladder represents an earlier period of time in Spain's history. The castle is destroyed by the termites, and the characters renounce their previous greed and hypocrisy, affirming their new identities. Working together, they reconstruct a new Tower of Babel. Latidia and the Martian Pilgrim embrace rapturously; she is spiritually restored, and the work ends on a note of melodramatic affirmation.

As Arrabal has demonstrated in a number of previous works,[53] the resolution of destructive forces which leads to fulfillment through transcendence can only occur via a direct confrontation with man's basest, most depraved thoughts and deeds. Seeking the salvation of his native country, the author logically depicts its ills in a provocatively grotesque and shocking manner. The termites which effect the destruction of the castle are at once a symbol of Spain's rotting traditions and a Surrealist metaphor of the rejuvenation through art of the country's spirit. To attain greatness, Spain must first destroy systematically, from within, its hypocritical pride and its false heroes. By assigning the roles of Spain's greatest historical figures to grotesque characters, Arrabal exposes the decadence he considers rampant in his country. By having those characters genuinely accept their identity at the end of the play, he affirms the greatness inherent in the Spanish people and their traditions — a latent greatness which will become meaningful only in a totally revitalized Spain.

Latidia, the play's protagonist, embodies emotions of the dramatist himself. Her blindness and alienation from herself and the greedy and hypocritical characters that surround her reflect Arrabal's relationship to his own country. She is a modern Don Quixote, a visionary who consoles herself with grandiose dreams of former national glory. The only thing that she can "see" are the words written on the eyes of the Martian Ass: "Love" and "Serenity." The animal comes to symbolize the magical quality of artistic inspiration; the full significance of those two words becomes clear when Arrabal has effected a catharsis making possible the optimistic ending on both aesthetic and thematic levels. At the beginning of the drama, Latidia tells the ass about the black pearl forcibly extracted from her neck by a priest.[54] Her mother, under instructions from the priest, had told her earlier that the pearl was poisoning her blood and corrupting her soul with vice and depravity. The ass helps to determine where the pearl has been hidden (in Latidia's mother's girdle); and at the conclusion of the work the Martian Pilgrim returns it to her neck. She is a complete person again; good and evil, purity and sensuality (the pearl had lain against her mother's sex organ for all of these years) fuse; the personal and the national levels resonate harmoniously. Arrabal's psychic wholeness — depicted through his protagonist — mirrors and complements his vision of Spain's rebirth. Latidia and the Martian fly above the stage and disappear at the end of the play; this visually suggests and evokes the symbol of the eagles, majestic birds which contrast sharply with the termites and represent the spirit and glory of the Spanish people.

Like *Today's Young Barbarians, The Tower of Babel* also contains a reference to class struggle. The hatred of the beggars for the aristocracy, underlying the beggars' need to dominate it, is made explicit in the thirteenth scene where the Cripple informs the Count that his grandfather had been publicly whipped for blasphemy as ordered by the then Count of Ecija. The drunkard then tells how his ancestor had been forced to wear a muzzle to prevent him from eating the olives he was picking. These expressions of class resentment are followed immediately by the appearance of Latidia and the Martian Pilgrim descending a ladder. In order to reconstruct a new, vibrant Spain, social equality must be affirmed. In the play's final scene, all of the characters ascend toward heaven together by climbing the Tower of Babel (which traditionally represents disharmony and lack of communication but has now been converted into a symbol of social, political and aesthetic unity).

The diverse forces examined and reconciled in *The Tower of Babel* require an equally disparate range of aesthetic and dramatic techniques. Lyricism and patriotic ardor clash with biting irony, pornography and the grotesque. The essential dialectic of the drama's style and content is depicted in the purely visual fourth scene in which Latidia's exaltation before the mummified heroes of Spain's past is juxtaposed with the Marquis' and the Hired Killer's donning of gas masks so as not to vomit from the odor. Caricature (the Hired Killer with his guns, Jaguar and Mafioso demeanor) and irony (having the role of el Cid played by a perverse cripple who makes a love slave of Doña Jimena, the Countess) culminate in the melodramatic affirmation of self and country concluding the work. The author's socio-political concern is communicated through Brechtian songs, such as the one-eyed beggar's satiric glorification of money.[55] In *The Tower of Babel,* Arrabal takes the spectator on an artistic journey through the depths of Spanish hypocrisy and internal strife to effect a catharsis making the drama's conclusion artistically and thematically justifiable.

The final period of Arrabal's dramatic production is character-ized by a new didactic thrust, a concern for socio-political ills throughout the world, but especially in Spain, and a search for ever new techniques for making a performance of one of his dramas a genuinely visceral experience. His stage directions place increas-ingly greater demands on stage designers as Arrabal attempts to expand what is possible in the medium of theater. Attenuation of his ability to turn the stage into a forum for projection of the fasci-nating, painful, and frightening inner world of his own psyche is compensated for, at least in part, by his use of provocative imagery and metaphors, his energetic commitment to his themes, and his union of all of the arts to create even more of a total theater than existed before. Arrabal, still a relatively young man, has utilized the stage in order to resolve his own inner conflicts and has finally gained the satisfaction of seeing his plays performed once again in his native country.[56] The question which now remains to be answered is: what direction will future endeavors take? Some ad-justment will have to be made in the thematic focus of his drama, but the vitality of the man and the fertility of his artistic imagina-tion are such that new innovative works for the theater can in any case be anticipated.

CHAPTER 5

The Novels

A LTHOUGH Fernando Arrabal is essentially a man of the theater, his intense need to express himself artistically has led him to experiment with other media. To date he has authored three novels. As with any experimental artist, traditional forms and genres have only limited significance. Arrabal's novels exhibit his poetic bent and give ample evidence of his dramatic orientation. Themes, motifs, and episodes from his plays are introduced into his prose fiction. All three of his novels consist of a series of brief chapters or vignettes structured in accordance with the author's acute sense of time and memory; the latter two demonstrate many precepts of Panic. This study as a whole reflects Arrabal's emphasis on theater; limitations of space allow only a brief consideration of his prose fiction and of its place in the schema of his total artistic production.

I Baal Babylone (Baal Babylon)

Baal Babylon, written in 1959, is Arrabal's most autobiographical work. Termed "one of the most haunting and terrifying evocations of childhood since Joyce's *A Portrait of the Artist as a Young Man,*"[1] it is written in a style which "might be likened to the pointillist technique in painting."[2] The novel consists of a series of short passages, or litanies, all narrated in the first person, "each of which transcribes or evokes a highly charged emotional experience or sensory impression."[3] No attempt is made to order chronologically the eighty vignettes constituting the work. The novel's point of view provides unity and dramatic impact to its diverse episodes. As Percy Lubbock has noted in his classic study of prose fiction, "This, then, is the readiest means of dramatically heightening a reported impression, this device of telling the story in the first per-

son, in the person of somebody in the book.''[4] Arrabal's narrator
(and counterpart) brings to the work an ingenuous point of view
which complements and, to a certain extent, helps to produce the
lyrical quality of its style. Poetic repetitions, musical prose, and
carefully conceived understatement combine with the events of the
novel to produce a dramatic tension resulting from the clash
between form and content. Thus, *Baal Babylon* succeeds in underscoring the bigotry and hatred which pervaded Arrabal's own
youth by treating them with "lyrical irony" rather than with natu-
ralistic ardor.

The picture of the author's youth emerging from the novel is a
disturbing and, at times, a horrifying one. Pain and cruelty per-
meate the boy's experiences with religion, school, and sexuality.
His Aunt Clara, a religious fanatic, effects a link between the concepts of religious penitence and eroticism in his mind; in one episode, she obliges him to beat her until she reaches sexual climax.
(Her "suffering" is endured ostensibly so that the soul of the boy's
deceased grandfather will enjoy a happier fate in the next life.) The
continuing retributions enacted against Republican sympathizers in
post-Civil War Spain are echoed in the cruelty of the young narrator's instructors in school and in the games his companions play.
The lyrical quality of Arrabal's prose and the naiveté of the narrator combine with the horror of events described to produce the sort
of dialectical tension frequently associated with the grotesque
mode. One example is the boy's description of a group of men executed by the regime: "Lying against the opposite wall were the
bodies with the bloody heads. The women were screaming and spit-
ting on the bodies. Aunt Clara threw a handful of sand on them,
hard. Then Elisa did the same thing; then me."[5]

The dominant presence in *Baal Babylon* is of the narrator's
mother. Her allure for him, self martyring outbursts, and persistent
attempts to eradicate all memory of her husband from the family
dominate much of the novel. She is essentially the same mother
character who appears in Arrabal's early play, *The Two Executioners.* But here she never indulges in hysterical, orgiastic sadism;
her sweetness, attractiveness, and ability to manipulate the feelings
of her son make her a less dramatic, but more credible and ultimately a more perfidious character. The young narrator's enumeration of the women who cannot compare with his mother comes late
in the novel with tremendous impact because of the author's care-
ful development of her character. It is climaxed by the following

statement: "No one, mama, was like you. I looked hard, mama, but no one was like you. No one had a tongue so wet or knees so white as you, mama. No one" (pp. 77–78). In light of the mother's repeated assertions of concern for her family, personal sacrifice for her children and her devious but pointed attacks against her incarcerated husband, her continuing influence over her son becomes agonizingly disquieting. The relationship between the two reaches its climax in the novel's final dialogue when she reassures the boy he will not grow up to be a Jew and an anarchist like his father. He then capitulates in a manner paralleling that of Maurice in *The Two Executioners,* declaring rapturously: "Then, mama, you said I was a good boy and you kissed me. Yes" (p. 104).

The essential element lacking in the boy's life (as portrayed in the novel) is the father. The young boy's inquisitiveness is consistently squelched by the mother's denigration of her husband: "I was the one who assumed responsibility for you and brought you up as well as I could. I'm the one who gave you everything he should have given you if he had acted like a good father" (p. 29). Despite the ending of the novel and the suffocating ubiquity of the mother, a note of hope does remain. It consists of the narrator's persistent longing to know more about his missing parent: "I don't know if he liked red like Elisa or blue like you, mama. / I don't know if he liked playing with the sand on the beach, mama. / I don't know if he liked walking around the harbor, mama. / I don't know if he made footprints in the snow and looked at them afterward or if he walked along the palm trees in Melilla on sunny days, mama" (p. 31). Arrabal's use of repetition in the above cited passage affirms the persisting influence of the man who haunts the dreams and subconscious memories of the boy. And his father's Dr. Plumb pipe, which the narrator smokes in a number of the novel's vignettes, comes to symbolize the pivotal role of the parent in the boy's psyche. The central tension in the novel then is the struggle between the two parents for control of their son's subliminal world. That there is no clear-cut victory can be construed as an affirmation of the hope that freedom and the spirit of inquiry will eventually contravene the hypocritical oppression of church and state incarnated by the mother.[6]

The title of the novel is integrated into its text near the conclusion when the mother seeks to convince her son that it is better that his father has died, since he deserved his fate: "Besides he was punished for his sins; don't forget that even God punishes the guilty; in the Bible it says: 'I shall punish Baal in Babylon' " (p. 101). As was noted in the analysis of *The Architect and the Emperor of Assyria,* Babylon is a Jungian symbol for the "mother of all abominations" who leads people into whoredom with her temptations. Symbolically, then, the title of the novel alludes to the mother's attempt, under the cloak of righteousness, to punish a man who differed with her beliefs and who sought to secure the allegiance of a younger generation.

Baal Babylon is a moving and disturbing work utilizing an appealing lyricism to contrast with and protest against the horrors to which the young Arrabal himself was subjected. Its eighty sections crystallize the most haunting memories of the author, interwoven with a picture of life in post-Civil War Spain. By presenting the action from a youthful perspective, the novelist adds dramatic impact and poignancy to a most efficacious first novel.

II   L'Enterrement de la sardine (The Burial of the Sardine)

The Burial of the Sardine (1960) anticipates a number of the precepts of Panic to be formulated a few years later. The title of the novel is taken from a painting by Francisco Goya and enunciates one important component of the work's aesthetic. Goya's painting depicts a carnival; but the gaiety normally associated with such an event is tempered, if not totally dispelled, by ominous dark clouds fused with the trees, swirling masses of people, a jeering face on the most prominent banner, and frightening figures and masks in the crowd. The spirit of the painting, with its emphasis on the agitation in the throng, constitutes the substance of the novel's odd numbered chapters. The even numbered ones focus on the first-person narrator, the dwarf Hieronymous, who describes the vertiginous activity below. Chained to the wall in his room overlooking the street, he is counseled, tortured and seduced by two girls, Altagore and Lis. Arrabal's identification with Hieronymous is implicit in the novel; his view of himself as a dwarf has been noted in published interviews. And the name, Hieronymous, introduces another painter, Bosch who, along with Goya, is considered a forerunner of Surrealism and proponent of the grotesque. There is an allusion to Bosch's masterpiece, "The Garden of Earthly Delights," in the fifty-first chapter where the dwarf describes a couple in the street, a sexually aroused male and a pig dressed in a nun's habit.[7] *The*

Burial of the Sardine then is a work steeped in the visual arts with a strong flavor of Surrealism. Calls for "Alice" and references to a "Reverend Dodgson" serve to introduce the third important influence on the aesthetic of the work: Lewis Carroll.[8] The entire work is subsumed by a dream-like quality; the violence of the street scenes grows in intensity throughout the novel until the seventy-fifth and final chapter where the two alternating threads of the work's plot fuse into a Surrealist nightmare at once intriguing, mysterious, and frightening.

The even numbered chapters of *The Burial of the Sardine* are reminiscent of *The Song of Barabbas*. The two women, Altagore and Lis, parallel Arlys and Sylda in the earlier play. The concept of man educated by woman in the ways of life prevails in both. Altagore teaches Hieronymous how to do a number of things, including: divine the future, interpret dreams and numbers, and kiss passionately. Hieronymous' education, like Giafar's, is directed toward preparing him for initiation into the liberated world of the artist. Eroticism is a central component of that world; Hieronymous is chained and whipped by the two women. He sometimes instigates their cruelty by pleading that they not do something to him, thus suggesting the torture to them (like Lis, in *Fando and Lis*). One of the women is a brunette, the other a blonde. Together they represent generic woman. The women symbolically fuse in one episode where they make love to one another. Lis, the blonde, appears in chapter sixty-eight as a man who, encouraged by Altagore, obliges Hieronymous to perform fellatio on her. This latter androgyne suggests the union of all contradictions which is the object of alchemy and Panic. Arrabal introduces into the novel all of his feelings of inadequacy through Hieronymous; by having the character break his chain to join the chaos and confusion of life in the street, Arrabal seems, on one level, to be affirming his liberation from psychic restraints and his entrance into and identification with the Panic world.

In the turmoil filled street scenes of the odd numbered chapters, certain figures, banners, and songs recur with mathematical precision. The Goyesque quality of the revellers is permeated with the grotesque in the form of creatures part man, part animal.[9] Arrabal also utilizes these chapters to introduce a note of socio-political criticism within the framework of his Surrealist vision. Religion is attacked through the hypocritical sadism of the flagellants and the bestial nature of the priests in procession. The latter devour long sandwiches between prayers as grease drips into their beards. They belch loudly and deal with suffering old people pleading for a poisoned host by kicking them aside (p. 51). The church's dependence on the military is affirmed by the Bishop who licks a general's boots. And the corruption of our commercialized culture is summarized by a banner with a picture of a huge tube of toothpaste and another that proclaims "Drink Coke."

The chapters presenting the street scenes are structured by an accelerating rhythm of destruction and perversity. Craters appear in the ground and bizarre, skeletal creatures emerge. The author's vision grows increasingly apocalyptic. Certain nameless characters which have appeared throughout figure prominently in the conclusion. A man who has been searching for his white cat with black spots is abruptly murdered. A mysterious old man with long white hair and black eyes who has frequently established eye contact with Hieronymous now summons him to the street. Before Hieronymous has unlocked his chain and been called by the old man, he watches the coffins of Lis and Altagore being pulled by two of the skeletal creatures. Corpses, fire, craters, scavengers, fights between animals, undulating reptiles, and other frightening beings and occurrences comprise the Boschian hell Hieronymous is poised to enter. The appearance of the two women in the street unites the novel's two plots into a vision of Surrealist chaos. Hieronymous' descent is an ambiguous act; it affirms his freedom, but leaves unresolved the question of his fate. Either Panic life or Panic death and hell or both may be symbolized by the street below. On the "personal" level, the author-protagonist's descent may not be a triumphant act, but the aesthetic vision it affirms serves as an announcement of the direction to be taken by Arrabal's writings during the 1960s.

Throughout *The Burial of the Sardine* Altagore periodically informs Hieronymous of what is to be the nature of his activities in the coming months. (The whole year represents his life.) She delays giving him the information for December until her final encounter with him, when she states: "In December the snow will fall in the fields and you will die alone" (p. 192). The linear component of the plot indicates then that Hiernymous' descent into the street is symbolic of his death (personified by the old man). But frequent repetitions in the work and the suggestion that the entire novel is the dream of its creator, Hieronymous, superimpose a circular structure.[10] In chapter fifty-eight, the narrator tells Lis of his dream in which she appeared with bare breasts and a white skirt with red and green pockets. At the end of the chapter, when Hieronymous looks up at Lis, she appears exactly as he had seen her in his dream. Illusion and reality fuse; *The Burial of the Sardine* projects an aesthetic vision which transcends existential questions by suggesting that freedom and self affirmation for its protagonist and for mankind can be attained through the power of Surrealist or Panic art.

III   Fêtes et Rites de la Confusion
(Rites and Celebrations of Confusion)

Arrabal's last and most complex novel, *Rites and Celebrations* (1967), is steeped in the philosophy and aesthetics of Panic. It was published in Spanish under the title, *Arrabal celebrando la ceremonia de la confusión* (*Arrabal Celebrating the Ceremony of Confusion*), and is the work which the writer had autographed leading to his arrest in his native Spain. Symmetry and mathematical precision govern its structure: it consists of six chapters, four of which (the first, second, fourth and fifth) contain nine "labyrinths" each, the third and sixth chapters being much briefer and limiting their perspective to the *"rond-point,"* or *"crossroads,"* where a gigantic statue of a woman is located. The novel as a whole has been described as "the exploration by a man of the labyrinth of his memory, where he rediscovers the obsessions that are at the same time those of all mankind, because memory is life."[11] Summarizing the content of all thirty-six "labyrinths" is beyond the scope of this study; a brief consideration of the structure, themes, symbols, and aesthetic of the novel will seek to relate it to the corpus of Arrabal's literary production and the tenets of Panic.

The principal focus of *Rites and Celebrations of Confusion* concerns the rebirth of the author-protagonist into the Panic world as a result of self exploration and analysis of himself and his art with the aid of memory power. The birth motif is central to the entire novel. The female giant at the crossroads — where past, present, and future, dream and reality, order and confusion all coalesce — represents the origin of life and the source of artistic inspiration. (The words LOVE and CHANCE can be seen in her eyes.) Her enormity reflects Arrabal's view of himself as dwarfed both physically and psychologically by women, but also serves to affirm the mythic dimension of the novel. The number nine alludes to the human gestation period, and the four series of nine labyrinths represent the seasons of the year. (The year symbolizes a human life; hence we are presented with a unit of time within a unit of time.)

The third and central chapter of the novel does not present the narrator's voyage through a series of nine labyrinths. What he views on the statue there gives no indication of where to enter the labyrinths (as happens in the other chapters), but consists instead of the words, "My Biography." Those words become a section of the chapter encompassing the narrator's mythic birth from out of the head of his mother.[12] In the following section, entitled "Love," he struggles to establish his own identity apart from that of "Her" and is introduced to art which is equated with the logic and patterns of chess. In the final section, "Anatomy," he explores his physical being, represented symbolically in the painting "Anatomy Explained by Arrabal."[13] At the conclusion of the section, "She" tells him that the painting he has been describing is a mirror. Art is life; and the narrator must continue to travel through the labyrinths of his own subconscious in the quest[14] to discover himself as man and artist.

The very first labyrinth in the novel identifies art with life. The narrator is at first unable to perceive anything at all on the canvases a mysterious lady shows him. When she urges him to utilize his memory in examining them, he sees two paintings reflecting the reality of his initial encounter with her. Reality, in the oneiric vision of the Surrealist artist, becomes an elusive concept. It fuses with the narrator's dream fantasies in the seventh labyrinth[15] and is reflected in a kaleidoscope of different forms in the twenty-third labyrinth where Arrabal's female companion is transformed into a myriad of reflectors.[16] Multiplicity of reality, reflected in the fingernails and eventually in the entire body of the girl, is reinforced as a concept in the following labyrinth when an architect lives and dies in many places and in many ways at the same time.

The guiding force which sustains the narrator on his arduous inner journey is memory. In the fourth labyrinth, he loses his ability to recall things but then retrieves it by drinking a liquid kept in a jar. Water, or the sea, becomes a symbol for dreams and memory in the novel. In the twenty-first labyrinth the narrator descends into the depths of the sea in search of his visage (his identity); he encounters all of his faces and also finds a mirror with ME inscribed on it. Through memory, he has found the path to himself. The liquid which symbolizes memory suggests amniotic fluid. Birth (or rebirth) and memory fuse into a single invigorating force; the narrator's self discovery has become possible only through reconstruction of the origins of thought (or the subconscious).

In the thirteenth labyrinth, a poet, suffering from the absence of animal passion, submits to an operation and discovers true ecstasy. The scene is reminiscent of the climax of *Ars Amandi;*[17] as indicated in my earlier analysis of the play, the narrator has experienced an alchemical transformation which will permit his ascension into the Panic realm of the marvelous where all dualities are resolved.

The aesthetic of *Rites and Celebrations* is strongly Surrealist. In the twentieth labyrinth, a mysterious little man presents the narrator with the image of an eyeball sliced by a razor. As in the film, *Un Chien andalou* (*An Andalusian Dog*) by Salvador Dalí and Luis Buñuel, the image symbolizes the penetration of superficial reality and entrance into the realm of the surreal. The novel is replete with surrealistic images and events. As with many of Arrabal's works, its aesthetic owes a great deal to the visual arts. In the labyrinths, the following artists are evoked directly: Botticelli, El Greco, Fragonard, Bosch, and Goya. Goya is identified as the master of Panic and confusion; when the narrator discovers that his brain has been devoured by a little dog, the animal's manifestation suddenly corresponds to the dog in a famous painting by Goya. Thus, the narrator's aesthetic is equated with that of the Spanish painter's.

With the aid of the force of memory and the aesthetic of Surrealist art, the narrator succeeds in arriving at the center of his own essence. "At the end of this journey through time and the self, there is a messianic vision of a domain of simultaneity, of metamorphosis, of omnipresence, of enlightenment and ecstasy, which depicts a time continuum in which past, present, and future, dream and reality coexist. It is at this point that the individual self merges with being."[18] Arrabal's ecstatic affirmation of the clairvoyant vision accruing to the artist who penetrates the realm of Panic constitutes perhaps his most positive declaration of the therapeutic power of art:

and I am happy, for I see and I know eternity, and my memory is enriched and I perceive the bird who, every hundred years, steals a drop of water from the sea, and I see the oceans dry up because of him, and I see the stones of the mountains, and all the sands of the beaches, and I understand life and I am cat, and Phoenix and swan, and elephant and child, and old man, and I love and am loved, and I discover shores and paradises, and I am here and there, and I possess the seal of seals and as I fall into the future I feel that ecstasy seizes me to never leave me again.[19]

Arrabal's three novels constitute a significant and intriguing offshoot from the mainstream of his artistic production. They confirm the poetic sensibility and the concepts of imagery and structure already associated with his theater. Their chronology allows the reader to follow, in miniature, the author's crystallization and incorporation of the tenets of Panic into his works. They demonstrate that the focal point of his inspiration, in all genres, is to be found in his search, within himself, for psychological and artistic wholeness, for the resolution of conflicting forces both in his own subconscious and in the realm of external reality. The Marxist critic, Georg Lukács, has stated: "The novel tells of the adventures of interiority; the content of the novel is the story of the soul that goes to find itself, that seeks adventures in order to be proved and tested by them, and, by proving itself, to find its own essence."[20] If Lukács' observation is a valid one, then Arrabal's desire to express himself in the genre of the novel is fully understandable.

CHAPTER 6

Miscellaneous Works

A S has been noted in previous chapters, Arrabal's dramas utilize music, dance, slides and projections, and also visual stage images deriving from the plastic arts. Although he has succeeded in converting some of his plays into spectacles uniting several of the arts, his adventurous bent and creative energies have also led him to attempt poetry, filmmaking, photography and the design of paintings (carried out by artists who work for him and follow his instructions). These endeavors, with the exception of the films, are of minor importance within the framework of his total artistic production; so this chapter will be proportionately brief in its consideration of these diverse works.

I   *The Films*

Arrabal's first film, *Viva la muerte (Long Live Death),*[1] was made in Tunisia in 1970 and premiered in Paris on May 12, 1971. Although Arrabal himself identifies *Baal Babylon* as its source, both the aesthetic and the *Weltanschauung* reflected by the film differ substantially from the novel.[2] During the eleven years between the works, Arrabal developed the concept of Panic, worked closely with the Surrealists in Paris, was incarcerated in Spain, and expanded significantly his concept of "baroque" and the use of the grotesque. *Long Live Death* preserves the basic structure of *Baal Babylon;* like the novel, it presents a series of autobiographically based vignettes that violate the dictates of ordinary chronology. But the film differs from the novel in its extensive use of dreams and nightmares which shatter the viewer's temporal and spatial orientation. The influence of Surrealism is evident in the film's focus on the subconscious dream-world of its protagonist, Fando. Arrabal developed an innovative filming technique for this work in

133

order to give the dream sequences their own visual identity and to
augment their impact upon the audience.[3]

Techniques and imagery from several of Arrabal's dramas are
integrated into *Long Live Death*. *The Two Executioners* provides
the film with one of its central episodes, the mother's denunciation
of her husband. However, the film transcends the aesthetic of the
early play and so gives evidence of Arrabal's continued artistic
growth. Baroque excesses such as the mother's marching about to
oriental dance music while her husband is being tortured and, in a
later scene, playing the violin as an accompaniment to his agonized
suffering, confirm this development. Another new and striking
image in the film shows the mother with her arms enveloped in
darkness and spread wide like the wings of a vulture, suggesting
that religion and tradition (incarnated by the female parent
throughout Arrabal's work) are sustained and nourished by death
rather than by life. Other images, some of which are adapted from
the more mature plays, acquire added impact in the medium of
cinema and allow Arrabal to achieve some stunning visual effects
that simply are not possible in the theater.

The integral role the grotesque is to play in the film is strikingly
foreshadowed by the series of drawings done by Roland Topor[4]
projected on the screen simultaneously with the delineation of the
cast and credits. These drawings are much in the style of Hieronymous Bosch or the Goya of "The Disasters of War"; they epito-
mize the generally accepted conception of the term "grotesque" in
their depiction of the mutilation and distortion of human beings.
The drawings also reflect a splitting asunder of our world and its
values through the frightening mixture of mechanical, vegetable,
animal, and human elements. They also foreshadow a number of
the images and themes in the film, some of which will be introduced
by the reappearance of a particular drawing. The primal position
they occupy in the film, then, is clearly justifiable in light of their
significance both to the technique and the content of *Long Live
Death*.

The grotesque images in *Long Live Death* are found principally
in its dream sequences. They appear with increasing rapidity in the
second half of the film and provide the work with an emotional and
aesthetic catharsis. In combination with Arrabal's utilization of
memory as a liberating force, the film communicates a feeling of
release, of escape from the mother's nefarious influence. The violent rupture of chronological time in the film has a counterpart in

the play, *The Garden of Delights*. The Panic concept of memory allows the filmmaker to project into the future and present a scene in which Fando is suddenly a young man in his twenties.[5] His mother demands that he castrate his father (in the form of a bull). He does so and presents her with the testicles which she ritualistically devours. She then sews her son into the bloody bull; this grotesque image clearly affirms her role as castrator, as well as ostensibly allowing her to fulfull amorous desires held toward the boy. The entire scene is presented in a manner consonant with Arrabal's view of theater (and film) as rite or ceremony.

The film's optimistic conclusion is justified by the violence of its catharsis which liberates the filmmaker from his psychic traumas, as well as by the frightening view of future possibilities contained in the sequence with the castrated bull. Fando, bandaged and weak after an operation for tuberculosis,[6] is wheeled off on a cart by his young girlfriend, Thérèse, in order to search for his father. The camera focuses on a scene which incorporates a touch of the incongruous humor of the Surrealists by the inclusion on the cart of Thérèse's pet turkey; then slowly and majestically the lens zooms upward toward the heavens. In this film, Arrabal attains a degree of spiritual and artistic liberation unsurpassed by any of his other works. *Long Live Death* constitutes a major achievement in the field of cinema, a remarkable accomplishment in light of the fact that it is Arrabal's first film.

Based on *The Architect and the Emperor of Assyria, J'irai comme un cheval fou* (*I Would Go Like a Crazy Horse*, 1973) is essentially a two character film.[7] Aden, pursued by guilt feelings deriving from his relationship to his mother (whom, it is hinted, he has killed), escapes from the western world and seeks refuge in the desert where he encounters Marvel. The latter, like the Architect, is a man of nature uncorrupted by civilization who controls the sun, the moon, and all of God's creatures. Aden persuades Marvel to accompany him to the city, but his attempts to introduce Marvel to the joys of politics, sex, and religion all end in failure; Aden is ultimately gunned down by police who have been seeking him in connection with the death of his mother. Marvel retrieves the body and wheels it to the desert in a cart; then, in a climactic ceremony of communion, he devours his friend's body, suffers the intense pain of childbirth, and metamorphoses into Aden-Marvel, rising into the red sky of the desert.

Like *The Architect and the Emperor of Assyria, I Would Go*

Like a Crazy Horse explores the relationship between past and present, the concepts of civilization and death, the impact of social forces on man's psyche, and the significance of human empathy and love. Only through death is Aden able to liberate himself from the stifling influence of his civilized past. As Angel Berenguer has noted in his analysis of the film: "This, precisely, is the originality of the author who transposes not the absurdity of Western Civilization, but the inviability of a culture that prevents all perspectives of realization for the individual, affirming, nevertheless, as definitive acquisitions, the liberties and privileges which, in reality, it denies" (p. 78).

Guérnica, Arrabal's latest film, was made in Italy in 1975. Although its title is the same as one of Arrabal's early dramas, it is not actually based on a specific play. (It does anticipate a few of the components of *The Tower of Babel,* however.) The film utilizes newsreels of the Spanish Civil War to reinforce its portrayal of the horror of the conflict and the brutality and hypocrisy of the Nationalists. The tree of Guérnica becomes a symbol of hope for a new and better Spain. Its miraculous survival during the bombing of the town of Guérnica is paralleled by the triumphant escape of the film's two protagonists, Goya and Vandale.

Goya, the son of the Count of Cerralbo, represents Spain's enlightened aristocracy. In Surrealism Goya finds a means of repudiating the superciliousness of his father; his lifestyle and outlandish pranks constitute his reaction against the previous generations' traditions.[8] He is complemented in his efforts by the peasant sorceress, Vandale. They first meet in Guérnica and are drawn to one another. Goya releases a flock of doves[9] before going to dance with Vandale. The two young people are about to introduce themselves formally when the bombs hit, delaying the introduction until the film's conclusion. They both go to Villa Ramiro where Vandale echoes the words of La Pasionaria in inciting the Republicans to defend the town which has become a national example for both sides. Goya, piloting a small plane, also contributes valiantly to the Republican cause. But the inevitable occurs; the defenses are routed through the intervention of foreign troops and the two protagonists are captured.

Other important characters in the film include Villa Ramiro's schoolmaster and a group of dwarfs. In a sense, *Guérnica* deals not only with the Civil War of 1936–1939, but also with Spain's religious war against the Moors that culminated in the battle of Gra-

nada in 1476.[10] The dwarfs come to represent a persecuted component of the Spanish people. This racial note is reinforced by the
playing of a Nazi song on the sound track as the Nationalists break
through the Republican defenses at Villa Ramiro. In the most dramatic episode of the film, the Nationalists celebrate their victory
with a bullfight. The bull consists of a wheelbarrow with bull horns
attached on the front, to which a dwarf has been strapped. The
bullfighter is a subhuman specimen who grunts rather than speaks;
and the dwarfs suffer the horror of the *banderillas*, the *pica*, and
finally the fatal sword thrust of a real bullfight. At the end of the
scene, five dead dwarfs are dragged away on a white sheet by soldiers wearing butcher's aprons while the audience— which consists
of priests, the military, aristocrats, and skeletons — applauds
mechanically. The nightmarish quality of this macabre scene
affirms Arrabal's ability to utilize Surrealist techniques in a
uniquely personal manner. The political statement the scene
encompasses has tremendous impact within the context of the film
as a whole.

An inspiring schoolmaster in Villa Ramiro is juxtaposed with traditional forces in Spanish society that strive for homogeneity of
thought as well as race. On the blackboard in his classroom, these
words are written: "The words that fly on the wings of doves will
reign throughout the world." When the Count of Cerralbo comes
to him for help during the early stages of the war when the Republicans have taken over Villa Ramiro, the teacher cannot turn the
Count away, but refuses all monetary compensation in keeping
with his own dictate: "Love yourself so that you can love your
neighbor." He is repaid for his humanity by being sentenced to
death for the murder of the Count. When the latter appears to
vindicate him, the Tribunal waits until the Count has departed
before changing the form of execution to garrotting; they reason
that anyone who managed to hide a count must have had influence
among the Reds.[11]

In the film's final sequence, Vandale escapes and rescues Goya
who has been brutally tortured. She drags him to the top of the hill
overlooking Villa Ramiro. There, with the sun in the background,
the two introduce themselves; Goya's wounds all disappear; they
embrace passionately to the accompaniment of celestial music.
Arrabal's melodramatic image affirms his hope for Spain's future,
a hope rooted in the love between human beings and the coopera-
tive efforts of the masses and the enlightened aristocracy.

II *Poetry*

In all of Arrabal's works, in all genres, it is evident that there is "a touch of the poet" about him. It manifests itself in his use of language, verbal images (heavily surrealistic), and in the subtler rhythms deriving from the structure of a play or even the individual stage pictures he creates and juxtaposes. As with all avant-garde artists, Arrabal is susceptible to the accusation that he eschews traditional forms because he cannot master them. As he explains, however, creative endeavors must constitute a challenge for him. These are the reasons why he chose to write one hundred sonnets (they will not be analyzed in this study, but another book of poetry by Arrabal demands critical consideration).

La Pierre de la Folie (*The Stone of Madness*, 1963) confirms the tenuous distinction between genres among Arrabal's works. Categorized as "poetry,"[12] *The Stone of Madness* is quite similar in form to the author's novels; but its sections are somewhat briefer and less interrelated, and the exact repetition of some of them imparts a lyrical rhythm to the work as a whole that is less evident in the other works. *The Stone of Madness* defies classification; it is clearly an Arrabalian work, however, with respect to its themes, its use of language, and its structure. Of course, once again the author is only interested in finding an appropriate form and aesthetic for his thematic concerns.

The Stone of Madness is subtitled "Livre Panique"; its themes, reliance on dream images, and central philosophy all identify the work strongly with the Panic Movement. The "stone" of the title is the Philosopher's stone. It symbolizes creative energy, the ability to transform the baseness of life into the gold of artistic creation. That act must be realized, however, in a dream state verging on insanity. Throughout *The Stone of Madness,* the author-narrator periodically depicts himself sitting at his desk struggling to find inspiration to write. The word on the blank sheet of paper in his typewriter which confronts him identifies what has always been Arrabal's source of inspiration: MOI (ME).

The stone appears a number of times in the book in differing forms. It is forcibly extracted from inside the narrator's neck by his mother and a priest (a sequence later repeated in *The Tower of Babel*). The stone is also the bubble (its ethereal form) which floats from his heart to his brain and back again, a phenomenon described several times throughout the work and in its opening and concluding sections. Finally, the stone appears in the nightmare sequence where the narrator is castrated under the mother's supervision and where his testicles are replaced by stones. Thus, sexuality and the mother are identified as central components of the product of artistic creation.

The mother figure again plays a pivotal role in the entire work. She has never been depicted in a more horrifying manner than in *The Stone of Madness*. Some of the episodes in which the mother appears are derived from Arrabal's theater;[13] in one instance, she kisses her son on the lips, which begin to bleed (as in *The Grand Ceremonial*). The most devastating and grotesque scene in the book is one in which the narrator murders his own mother, cuts the body up into little pieces and throws them into the sewers of the city. But even this depraved act fails to liberate him from her suffocating influence. The severed head denounces the narrator to the police; and when he runs away in terror, one of the legs trips him, a hand pins him down, and the head begins to laugh hysterically.

The Stone of Madness is replete with fascinating dreams and nightmares. They affirm the union of opposites so central to alchemy and Panic,[14] deal with the author's psychological complexes and self denigration, allude to a number of other autobiographical concerns, and reiterate motifs found throughout Arrabal's literary production. The book is somewhat lacking in focus although the perspective of the narrator, the strategic and poetic use of repetition, and the linkage of some of its central motifs do provide it with a semblance of unity. It is not one of Arrabal's more important works, but constitutes an intriguing and provocative application of the aesthetic and ideology of Panic.

III   *The Paintings*

Arrabal has commissioned twenty-two paintings to date; they are designed by one of the three artists with whom he works (Felez, Arnaiz and Crespo). Arrabal himself once tried to paint, but was dissatisfied with the results. He refused, however, to deny himself the opportunity to communicate in yet another artistic medium. His source of inspiration for the paintings is often a simple, mundane element of reality,[15] but the final product manifests the oneiric quality, mythic dimension, humor, and intrigue associated with his literary works. As has been noted, several paintings have been integrated into his novel, *Rites and Celebrations of Confusion*, and were, in fact, considered in the analysis of the work. A description and analysis of all of the paintings is beyond the scope of this study. It will suffice to briefly present two of the most intriguing and representative ones.

Arrabal Combatting his Megalomania is dominated by the central figure of the author mounted on horseback and attired in a lavish costume. In the upper right hand corner there is a prison window through which a pair of hands reaches out imploringly to the figure of the author. An enormous body of water crosses the entire canvas. A phantom ship is discernible on it; emerging from the water are a hand holding a glass of champagne, a tree with a woman's breasts, a series of numbers, and a banner with the words LOVE, LIBERTY, and POETRY. In the lower portion of the painting, from left to right, are the following: a reproduction in miniature of Goya's *The Burial of the Sardine*, a severed column whose base is inscribed with the name "Arrabal," a group of naked children standing on their hands, a strange looking dog, and some men with penguin heads skating on the ice. The words on the tree define the artist's values, the Goya painting his aesthetic, and the prisoner's hands his psychological heritage (from his father). The artist's success is represented by the majesty of the steed he is riding. He seems oblivious to his surroundings; the title of the painting may well be a reminder to himself to maintain contact with the roots of his artistic inspiration.

Arrabal Celebrating the Ceremony of Confusion presents the author, garbed in a striped scarf and a robe, playing chess. A horde of monkeys invading his room through a stone window frame is climbing over his books which are all titled *Pan*. The far side of the chessboard is changing into a grassy field (divided into squares) with a bare tree. Flasks and bottles suggest experimentation of the alchemist. In the background, behind a large window, is a checkerboard floor with chess pieces occupying some of its squares. The painting captures the essence of the Panic vision, with its patterns, repetitions, logic and structure of chess, and hint of alchemy. Its title is the same as the Spanish version of *Rites and Celebrations of Confusion;* together with the novel, it is perhaps Arrabal's most direct artistic representation of Panic.

IV *Documents*

Under classification of "Documents," Arrabal's publisher,

Christian Bourgois, includes four of Arrabal's works. They are the following: *Letter to General Franco, Le Panique* (discussed in the chapter *Panic Theater*), *On Fischer: Initiation to Chess,* and *Arrabal's New York.* The *Letter to General Franco,* dated March 18, 1971, and published bilingually in French and Spanish, is a moving document in which the author utilizes a lyrical style, irony and sarcasm, and controlled form of understatement to give vent to feelings about Franco's reign of oppression in Spain. "Without the slightest degree of hatred or rancor, I must tell you that you are the man who has caused me the most harm"[16] is the statement opening the author's attack on the oppressive atmosphere created by Franco's regime in the name of order and religion. The document links Franco with the Spanish tradition of the Inquisition and its persecution of human beings. Childhood memories, prison experiences, and the horror of Civil War and post-Civil War Spain are all denounced in a controlled style which clashes with the horror of the *Letter's* content and serves to artistically underscore the intense feelings of the author about his country. The anguish felt by Arrabal reaches its zenith in the following accusation and protest directed to the Spanish dictator: "Your government, your censors, who had rotted my lungs and taken my father from me, prevented me from doing that to which I believed I had more right than a tree to the earth: writing in my own language" (p. 169).

On Fischer presents a brief biography of Bobby Fischer and seeks to justify Arrabal's interest in chess which he links with drama. It then presents the basics of the game, and concludes with a lengthier section analyzing the twenty games played by Fischer and Spassky during their historic confrontation in 1972.

Arrabal's New York utilizes captioned photographs taken by the author to subjectively project the essence of the city. The photos and words encompass a broad perspective, from Off-Off Broadway theater (Ellen Stewart's La Mama theater) to garbage cans and destitute old people; from cultural sophistication (a poster of Samuel Beckett) to the waiters at Ratner's who insist that you finish the goulash; from tenements and children playing in the streets to international restaurants and Shea Stadium. The book projects vividly the author's love for the city;[17] but it is Arrabal's desire to communicate feelings which has given him impetus to experiment with yet another art form: photography. His artistic sensibility is such that his ventures into new-found media are always interesting and sensitive even when lacking in technical expertise.

CHAPTER 7

Conclusions

T HE inherent tension of much the work of Fernando Arrabal
reflects the essence of his own personality; the author's deep-
seated internal conflicts are transformed into dialectical forces
structuring his work and augmenting dramatic impact. As Arrabal's artistic production evolved, another source of dualism and
tension surfaced in his work: the struggle within the author between
a tendency to rely on established themes and techniques, and a
desire to experiment with innovations. In *Interviews with Arrabal,*
the author relates the anecdote to Alain Schifres of how his wife
repeatedly and regretfully informed him that his latest literary
endeavor was invariably very much like his previous ones, that the
author's personality and subjective concerns still constituted the
singular essence of his work.[1] Her observation is true to some
degree for virtually everything he has written. Yet paradoxically,
when one compares Arrabal's earliest dramas to his most recent
ones, the evident degree of development and artistic growth is
remarkable.

The basic set of constants in Arrabal's dramatic writing includes
the following: clash between style and content, a close identification between the author and his protagonists, the oneiric quality of
his dramas' atmosphere, a structure based on cycles, repetitions,
antinomies, and metamorphoses, and the development of themes
having resonances on both psychological and political levels. The
central objective in all his work can best be summarized in one
word: "liberation" (both artistic and personal). Arrabal's unique
ability to convert the stage into a world of dreams and of subconscious desires — and to use music, light, slides, projections, and
stage pictures to engage, if not assault, the audience through the
mind's eye — has enabled him to produce a theater which (despite

its affinity to Surrealism, the Absurd, and the Artaudian "Theater of Cruelty") is still uniquely his own.

This study has traced the evolution of Arrabal's theater from incipience to its present form. Although Arrabal's dramatic production has been separated into three distinct periods, it should be apparent that such divisions are useful only as organizational guidelines, not inviolable categories. The essence of Panic can be identified throughout plays of all three "periods," although its role in his theater is much more decisive during the years following foundation of the Panic Movement. Arrabal, who with only a relatively small number of exceptions (mostly during the final period of his writing) has followed his enduring instincts with respect to both his source of inspiration and methodology of implementing the creative impulse, has kept the artistic level of his plays consistently high.

Any evaluation as to the merit of an author's work is of necessity largely subjective. And the obstacles to the appraisal of a living and active writer are enormous. In this study, emphasis has been placed on explicating each individual work and elucidating the integral relationship between thematic content and the writer's style, concept of structure, and overall technique. Judgmental statements have been rendered on occasion, both directly and indirectly (through the proportionate length of the analysis of each work). These should be viewed only as one critic's attempt to identify the most significant works — those which can be expected to have the greatest impact on future dramatists.

Two salient questions about the future emerge from this consideration of the complete works of Fernando Arrabal. Will his theater have lasting significance? Or will it prove to be of interest only so long as the political conditions in Spain which inspired so much of Arrabal's work remain unchanged? What position will be accorded to the dramatist when the development of drama in the second half of the twentieth century is evaluated and analyzed? A propitious perspective for the consideration of the second question is still remote at the present time. But the fascinating nature of the inner world Arrabal projects onto the stage promises to assure a continuing interest in his theater. The political component of his drama frequently does acquire a universal dimension which, as long as tyranny and oppression exist anywhere in the world, will make his drama relevant; and his work will certainly serve as an artistic documentation of a fascinating period in Spanish and world history.[2] It is difficult even to conjecture as to the thematic content of Arrabal's future plays, but his achievement in that genre is already such that new endeavors will be awaited with keen anticipation by Hispanists, Francophiles and students and critics of modern drama. That in itself is a major accomplishment in light of the dramatist's age and the obstacles that he has had to surmount during his formative years.

Notes and References

Chapter One

1. Alain Schifres, *Entretiens avec Arrabal* (Paris: Editions Pierre Belfond, 1969), p. 11.

2. Arrabal presents and/or refers to this image frequently in interviews and creative works. It receives its most emotional presentation in the short article, "Fernando Arrabal Ruiz, Mon Père," written in January, 1967, for the Spanish press, but denied publication by the censors. It appears in Schifres' *Entretiens* in a section at the end of the book entitled "textes annexes" (appended texts).

3. He remained under a death sentence for eight months; then his sentence was commuted to thirty years imprisonment. While incarcerated in Burgos he went insane and, on January 28, 1942, escaped from the psychiatric ward in his pajamas. There were three feet of snow on the ground at the time; he has never been heard from since.

4. Schifres, p. 15.

5. Ciudad Rodrigo is given the fictitious name of Villa Ramiro in both the novel, *Baal Babylone* (1959), and Arrabal's most recent film, *Guérnica* (1975).

6. Arrabal considered himself to be a dwarf with an immense head; he always felt that people were laughing at him. The words "head" and "size" could not be uttered in his presence without provoking an hysterical reaction (Schifres, p. 26).

7. Arrabal recounts the traumatic episode when his brother was locked up in a tiny room for four days and four nights by the Brothers at the San Anton School (Schifres, p. 19). This excessive cruelty seemed to him to be a corollary of the Brothers' fascism and of the atmosphere of hatred dominating post-Civil War Spain. The echo of political repression felt in the world of the children in Spain is a *bête noire* of Arrabal's reiterated throughout his work and constituting one of the most salient and poignant criticisms of the Franco regime in his *Carta al General Franco* (Paris: Union Générale d'Éditions, 1972). Consult pages 157–58 (of the Spanish text) of that "letter" for a presentation of the violence and cruelty dominating the Spanish schools and reflected in the games the schoolchildren played.

8. The most illustrious example would be Federico García Lorca.

9. The question of whether his mother actually denounced his father to the police remains unresolved although in light of the suddenness of the outbreak of the Civil War, it would appear to be quite unlikely. However, there is conclusive evidence that the content of the letters which she sent to her imprisoned husband was so demeaning of him that the prison officials stopped delivering them out of sympathy for him. She also denied him the opportunity of bidding farewell to his own children when she took the family from Melilla to Ciudad Rodrigo.

10. Arrabal completed virtually all of the work but never actually received the law degree.

11. The play is known in English as *Picnic on the Battlefield,* a translation of its French title *Piquenique en campagne.*

12. As the noted psychoanalyst Theodore Reik has observed: "What pushes us to love is thus an effort to escape from internal discontent. It takes the place of an original striving for self-perfection and is related to ambition. To be in love fulfills this aspiration and is felt as an achievement" (*Of Love and Lust: On the Psychoanalysis of Romantic and Sexual Emotions,* New York: Bantam Books, 1967, p. 29).

13. Arrabal would approve of the use of the term "corollary"; he likens writing to solving a chess problem. Moreover, the structure of some of his works reflects the development of a game of chess. Arrabal has become an outstanding chess player. He generally spends several hours a day working on chess problems. He has published a number of articles on chess in *L'Express* and has authored a book about Bobby Fischer and his match with Boris Spassky (*Sur Fischer,* Paris: Éditions du Rocher, 1974).

14. These included Belgium, Holland, Germany and the United States. A substantial amount of his time during these years was devoted to the study of chess.

15. These were Alexandro Jodorowsky and Roland Topor. For a consideration of the Panic Movement and the role of its founders and followers consult Fernando Arrabal's *Le Panique* (Paris: Union Générale d'Éditions, 1973).

16. As Arrabal has pointed out, the French critics actually made his reputation despite the intensity of their hostility because they helped to establish him as a provocative and controversial figure and thus, indirectly, aided him in attracting an audience.

17. The three painters with whom Arrabal has worked are Felez, Arnaiz and Crespo.

18. Arrabal could have received from six to twelve years in prison for his "crime." For a more detailed account of his experience in Spain, consult either Schifres, pp. 44–55, or Charles Marowitz's "Arrabal's Theater of Panic," *The New York Times Magazine,* December 3, 1972.

19. Arrabal is no longer sure himself if he wrote "Patra" or "Patria." He is certain that he intended to write the latter, but he feels that it is possible that his subconscious fear may have caused him to omit unknowingly

the "i." His explanation of this is found in Françoise Raymond-Mundschau's *Arrabal* (Paris: Éditions Universitaires, 1972), p. 27.

20. My translation of a statement made by Arrabal to Françoise Espinasse in an interview published in *Théâtre III* (Paris: Christian Bourgois, 1969), p. 11.

21. One example: A bullfighter was incarcerated for six years for having blurted out the statement "All Spaniards are cuckolds" in a fit of pique.

22. At that production, couples were separated, whips were distributed among members of the audience, and some spectators were even bitten by actors. A detailed description of the proceedings is contained in the Marowitz article previously cited.

23. The culmination might well be Clive Barnes' review of a production of *The Architect and the Emperor of Assyria* which appeared in the *New York Times* on Sunday, May 30, 1976. In the article Barnes alluded to a previous failure to fully understand the play on his part and praised both the work and Tom O'Horgan's direction of it at La Mama Theater.

24. As of October, 1976, at least ten completed dissertations have been devoted to Arrabal in the United States alone.

25. Marowitz, p. 40.

26. As of February, 1977, a total of thirty-six plays have been published.

27. Schifres, p. 45.

28. Schifres, p. 97.

29. This author witnessed ample evidence of this during the hours spent with Arrabal in New York City on May 29, 1976. It would be superfluous and imprudent to cite specific examples; suffice it to say that the time spent with Arrabal was thoroughly stimulating and entertaining.

30. Lorca was also known as the "life of the party," using his abilities to recite verses and accompany himself on guitar or piano as a means of attracting an audience. Yet he was also known to walk the streets of New York City after midnight as a means of dealing with his incessant fits of melancholy.

31. Schifres, p. 129.

32. He said the following to Bettina Knapp: "Strangely enough it is through the visual that I am inspired to write. I first see my idea and then I organize it dramatically" (*First Stage*, VI, 4 [Winter 1967–1968], p. 198).

33. Marowitz, p. 101.

34. Schifres, pp. 159–61. Arrabal decided to write one hundred sonnets precisely because the sonnet form, with its rigid structure, represented a challenge to him.

35. The pattern has changed several times. After working in French for a while, Arrabal went back to initiating his work in Spanish. He continues to favor the latter as his language for literary creation.

Chapter Two

1. The best known example is Martin Esslin's classic study of a group of contemporary playwrights for which he coined the expression "Absurd" to define both their basic philosophy and dramatic methodology. The term has become so widely accepted that it is sometimes forgotten that the authors now commonly referred to as Absurdists had themselves never heard it when writing their most significant plays. The edition of Esslin's book utilized for this study is *The Theater of the Absurd,* Revised Edition (New York: Anchor Books, 1969).

2. Esslin, p. 296.

3. And as Nahma Sandrow has indicated, the Surrealist perspective is also closely allied to that of the child: "The surrealists' characteristic mode was 'le merveilleux' — the marvelous — which signified to them a gleeful freedom of the imagination, a general liberation and purification within an acceptance of material reality, and a capacity for childlike wonder and fresh response," *Surrealism: Theater, Arts, Ideas* (New York: Harper and Row, 1972), p. 19. The best study of Arrabal's theater in light of the characteristics of Surrealism is John Killinger's article "Arrabal and Surrealism," *Modern Drama,* 14 (1971), pp. 210–23.

4. Arrabal relates a desire, early in his career, to limit the vocabulary in his plays to three hundred words (Alain Schifres, *Entretiens avec Arrabal — Inverviews with Arrabal* [Paris: Éditions Pierre Belfond, 1969] p. 163). This characteristic of his style also confirms his debt to Lewis Carroll, whose *Alice in Wonderland* and *Through the Looking Glass* had such a strong influence on him.

5. Schifres, p. 106.

6. *Ibid.,* p. 64.

7. Robert Brustein, *The Theater of Revolt* (Boston: Little Brown and Co., 1962), p. 12.

8. This tendency is common among the Surrealists, as Sandrow indicates in the following statement: "And the surrealist artist's own personality, dramatized, generally dominated his own work" (p. 35).

9. "Arrabal's Mother Image," *Kentucky Romance Quarterly,* 15 (1968), pp. 285–92.

10. Françoise Raymond-Mundschau, *Arrabal* (Paris: Éditions Universitaires, 1972), p. 103.

11. José M. Polo de Bernabé, "Arrabal y los límites del teatro," *Kentucky Romance Quarterly,* 22 (1975), p. 462.

12. As E. T. Kirby explains in his introduction to the critical anthology he entitled *Total Theater* (New York: E. P. Dutton & Co., 1969), the term "total theater" owes its origin to Richard Wagner and his concept of a *Gesamtkunstwerk,* or "total artwork." The term relates to Arrabal's mature theater both in the nontechnical sense of the word, suggesting a more complete involvement of the audience and as Kirby uses it (Arrabal

makes increasingly greater use of music, slides, dance and stage movement as his theater evolves).

13. "Wit and Its Relation to the Unconscious," in *The Comic in Theory and Practice* (New York: Appleton-Century Crofts, Inc., 1960), p. 78.

14. Geneviève Serreau, "A New Comic Style: Arrabal," *Evergreen Review,* No. 15 (1960), p. 62.

15. The efficacy of the sort of stage humor elucidating the dark side of life has been noted by J. L. Styan in his book *The Dark Comedy* (Cambridge: The University Press, 1968). As he perceptively comments in analyzing the discomfort in its audience contemporary theater often produces: "Clashing tears and laughter are uncomfortable companions, but, where in life their reconciliation is necessary if we are to make peace with ourselves, in drama their conflict is serviceable if that peace is to be disturbed" (p. 282).

16. Gloria Orenstein, *The Theater of the Marvelous: Surrealism and the Contemporary Stage* (New York: New York University Press, 1975), p. 153. Ms. Orenstein presents and analyzes the prime features of black humor as it functions in theater in her book (pp. 150–57).

17. Martin Esslin states: "As the incomprehensibility of the motives, and the often unexplained and mysterious nature of the characters' actions in the Theater of the Absurd effectively prevent identification, such theater is a comic theater in spite of the fact that its subject-matter is sombre, violent and bitter. That is why the Theater of the Absurd transcends the categories of comedy and tragedy and combines laughter with horror" (p. 361).

18. Esslin, p. 365.

19. Schifres, p. 114.

20. *Anatomy of Criticism* (Princeton: Princeton University Press, 1957), p. 105.

21. Carl Jung, *Psyche and Symbol* (New York: Doubleday Anchor Books, 1958), p. 11.

22. "El sentido de la obra de Arrabal," *Estreno,* II, No. 1 (1975), p. 13.

23. "From Tweedledum and Tweedledee to Zapo and Zepo," *Romance Notes,* XV, No. 2 (Winter, 1973), pp. 217–20.

24. *Picnic on the Battlefield* in *Guérnica and Other Plays* (New York: Grove Press, Inc., 1969), p. 111. All subsequent quotes from this play will be taken from the same edition.

25. *Das Groteske und das Absurde in Modernen Drama* (Stuttgart: W. Kohlhammer Verlag), p. 16.

26. "Forbidden Games: Arrabal," *Yale French Studies,* 29 (1962), p. 116.

27. In this work Arrabal bases the names of his characters on his own (Fernando — Fando) and his wife's (Luce — Lis). Variations on those names will appear frequently in subsequent plays.

28. As Janet Díaz suggests in her article, "Theater and Theories of Fer-

nando Arrabal," *Kentucky Romance Quarterly,* 16 (1969), pp. 143–54, this situation parallels that of the Red Queen's in Lewis Carroll's *Through the Looking Glass.* The Queen must run as fast as her legs will carry her if she wants to remain in the same spot.

29. *Fando and Lis* (London: John Calder, 1962), p. 47.

30. For an analysis of the phenomenon of projection as it relates to the *anima* and the *animus,* consult Jung's *Psyche and Symbol,* pp. 9–22. Jung's theories are applied to Arrabal's plays by Raymond-Mundschau, pp. 92–95.

31. For a consideration of the cultivation of sado-masochism as a natural corollary to the strict Catholic upbringing in Spain, consult Arrabal's *Carta al general Franco (Letter to General Franco)* (Paris: Union Générale d'Editions, 1972) or Arturo Barea's chapter on sexuality in Spain in *Lorca, The Poet and His People* (New York: Harcourt Brace, 1949).

32. Ortega, p. 11.

33. Schifres, p. 121.

34. The Dramatic World of Fernando Arrabal" Ph.D. diss., Syracuse University 1974, p. 172.

35. Consult the first chapter of Orenstein's book for a consideration of the deeper significance attached to the reversal of letters.

36. Díaz, p. 149.

37. Luce's inability to cry at the funeral adds a note of existential guilt to the play and is suggestive of Albert Camus' *The Stranger.* Arrabal's penchant for the grotesque is combined with his frequently used motif of the "innocent" criminal act when Vincent and Jerome describe the races they had with a legless cripple on a cart and how they murdered him when he refused to continue playing with them.

38. Schifres, p. 124.

39. *Ibid.,* p. 94.

40. *Irony and Drama* (Ithaca: Cornell University Press, 1971), p. 77.

41. Thomas Donahue, "Three Stages on Arrabal's Way" Ph.D. diss., University of Pennsylvania 1973, p. 36.

42. *Franz Kafka: Parable and Paradox* (Ithaca: Cornell University Press, 1966), p. 160.

43. Politzer, p. 162.

44. A term first used by Ramón Menéndez Pidal to describe the ideological division that can be identified as early as the eighteenth century in Spain and that intensifies until the climactic Civil War of 1936.

45. The state's representatives, as in *The Tricycle,* are unable to communicate with their victims. Lois Messerman suggests the possibility that their silence reflects the passivity of those who permit them to exist "The Theater of Fernando Arrabal: A Garden of Earthly Delights" Ph.D. diss., Ohio State 1970, p. 85.

46. Serreau, pp. 64–65. At a performance of the play by The Puerto Rican Traveling Theater Company in New York City on March 14, 1975, the audience supported this theory of the grotesque by laughing loudly and

uncomfortably at the hypocritical sadism disguised in the mother's asser-
tion that salt and vinegar will be medically beneficial for her spouse.

47. In working with Arrabal on a production of this play at Lock
Haven State College on February 15, 1977, he asked that the original
recording (Louis Armstrong's "Black and Blue") be changed to the
"Lacrymosa" section of the Berlioz *Requiem*. As he explained, when the
play was written, the Armstrong music, which was new to Europe, had a
mysterious, frightening quality about it; today that is no longer true, and
the Berlioz piece, played very loudly at the beginning and end of the play,
achieves a much more desirable effect.

48. *Orison* in *Four Plays* (London: John Calder, 1962), p. 11. All
subsequent references to this play will be taken from this edition.

49. This play has also been published in English under the title *The
Automobile Graveyard*. When plays have been published in Spanish I am
using the Spanish title since, for the most part, that is the original language
in which they were written. French titles will be used only when the Spanish version has not been published or is relatively inaccessible.

50. Frederick Hegel, *The Phenomenology of the Mind* (New York:
Harper and Row, 1967). For a more thorough application of Hegel's theo-
ries to several of Arrabal's plays, particularly *Fando and Lis* and *The Car
Cemetery*, consult Donahue's unpublished dissertation.

51. *The Car Cemetery* in *Four Plays* (London: John Calder, 1962),
p. 103.

52. Ortega, p. 12.

53. One of the most spectacular and exciting productions of an Arrabal
play was Victor García's staging of *The Car Cemetery* in Dijon, France,
during June of 1966. The *mise-en-scène* utilized parts of cars throughout
the theater; the spectators were seated on swivel chairs and all separation
between actors and audience was eliminated. In addition to converting the
entire theater into a stage, García interspersed performances of several
short Arrabal plays with *The Car Cemetery* [*Orison, The Two Executioners* and *La Communion solennelle (First Communion)*].

54. Two plays have been omitted from this otherwise complete
presentation, in chronological order, of Arrabal's theater. *Orchestration
Théâtrale* (1957), later revised and titled *Dieu tenté par les mathématiques
(God Tempted by Mathematics)* , is a work without dialogue using music,
light and various geometric shapes and figurations. I have not seen it performed and find it pointless to attempt an analysis of the piece on the basis
of stage directions, which constitute eighty-two pages. Moreover, Arrabal
has totally repudiated the work, terming it an interesting experiment that
failed. Although *Les Quatres Cubes (The Four Cubes*, 1960) does utilize
actors, it is also an abstract, mime piece lying outside the mainstream of
Arrabal's theater in all but its theme. Since Arrabal is so prolific, I have
found it expedient also to forego an analysis of this play.

55. *The Impossible Loves* in *The Drama Review,* 13 (1968), p. 86.

56. Schifres, p. 32.

57. Arrabal's recollection of his father covering his young son's feet with sand on the beach at Melilla is of great importance to him and should be considered in analyzing his works.

58. Orenstein, p. 124.

59. This play was published in Spain under the title *Ciugrena,* an anagram indicative of the impact of censorship on all phases of theatrical activity in the country.

60. The myth concerns the indestructible tree of Guérnica under the branches of which Basque kings have been crowned for centuries.

61. Similarities include Lira's use of the silent treatment and Fanchou's undressing Lira so that his friends can touch her.

62. "Arrabal and the Myth of Guérnica," *Estreno,* II, No. 1 (1975), p. 17.

63. Although Brecht's epic theater is fairly far removed from Arrabal's basic concept of drama, both playwrights do utilize dialectical tensions and ambiguities in some of their works; their vision of war in these two plays shares this tendency.

64. Kronik, p. 18.

65. Schifres, p. 56.

66. As Serreau states in her previously cited article: "There is in his work an incredible hunger for hope, an appetite we do not find, for example, in Beckett, of find no longer" (p. 62).

67. There are several manuscripts of the play; although it was published in 1959, the earliest version, a much shorter work, was written, according to David Whitton, in December, 1956. For an analysis of the evolution of the play from earliest form to published script of 1959, consult Whitton's article, "A Critical Edition of the Manuscript of the First Version of Arrabal's *Bicyclette du condamné," Forum for Modern Language Studies,* IX (1973), 253–68.

68. Schifres, p. 123.

69. Consult Beverly De Long-Tonelli's article "Bicycles and Balloons in Arrabal's Dramatic Structure," *Modern Drama,* 14 (1971), 205–09, for an analysis of this play which illustrates the relationship between structure and theme through a consideration of the play's dramatic symbols.

70. Raymond-Mundschau, p. 60.

71. *The Condemned Man's Bicycle* in *Plays,* Vol. 2 (London: Calder and Boyars, 1967), p. 136.

72. Messerman, p. 86.

73. *Fernando Arrabal* (Paris: Éditions Seghers, 1970), p. 63.

Chapter Three

1. An historical outline of the Panic Movement, written by Dominique

Sevrain and dated October 12, 1972, is contained in Arrabal's *Le Panique,* pp. 9–14.

2. *Le Panique,* p. 97.

3. The lecture appears in French in *Le Panique,* pp. 37–53, and in Spanish in a collection of plays, including *El cementerio de automóviles, Ciugrena* and *Los dos verdugos* (Madrid: Taurus, 1965).

4. *Le Panique,* p. 52.

5. As such, it is reminiscent of Lope De Vega's *El arte nuevo de hacer comedias* (*The New Art of Writing Plays,* 1609) despite the obvious differences in style between the two. Both tease the reader by making it difficult to reject or take entirely seriously the theories they present.

6. *Le Panique,* p. 99.

7. *Ibid.,* p. 47.

8. *Ibid.,* p. 98.

9. As Arrabal explains, because of his utilization of the concept of chance, the artist is the only man on earth capable of clarifying what is unforeseen: the future (*Le Panique,* p. 48).

10. As Gloria Orenstein states in her book *The Theater of the Marvelous* (New York: New York University Press, 1975), "Sexual perversions are chosen as the symbolic weapon for the attack on the institutions of church and state because they underline the human right to pleasure upon which Sadian morality is based" (p. 231).

11. *Loc. cit.*

12. *The Theater of the Absurd* (New York: Anchor Books, 1969), p. 353.

13. Orenstein, p. 54.

14. *Ibid.,* p. 55.

15. Arrabal worked with me in staging the two short plays *Orison* and *Solemn Communion* at Lock Haven State College on February 15, 1977. The experience provided me with direct insight into his concept of theater and theater production.

16. *Plays,* Vol. III (London: Calder and Boyars, 1970), p. 99. All subsequent references to this work will be taken from this same edition.

17. "Dialogue with Arrabal," *Evergreen Review,* No. 15 (1960), 70–75.

18. See José Ortega's study, "El sentido de la obra de Fernando Arrabal," *Estreno,* Vol. II, No. 1 (1975), 11–12, for an analysis of the role of "la madre natural" ("the natural mother") in the psyche of the playwright.

19. Françoise Raymond-Mundschau, *Arrabal (Paris:* Éditions Pierre Belfond, 1969), p. 128.

20. Alain Schifres, *Entretiens avec Arrabal* (Paris: Editions Pierre Belfond, 1969), p. 128.

21. The play was originally published in 1964 under the title *Le Couronnement* (*The Coronation*). It appears in revised form under its new title in Volume IV of Arrabal's *Théâtre* (Paris: Christian Bourgois, 1969).

This is the edition utilized for this study; for purposes of chronology however, the date of the earlier version was used.

22. "Approaches to Theory/Criticism," *Tulane Drama Review*, X (1966), 20–53:

23. *Ibid.*, p. 46.

24. As Orenstein states (p. 247), this idea had been advocated by André Breton in *Arcane 17.*

25. Orenstein, p. 247.

26. The importance of alchemy and the symbol of the androgyne to Surrealism in general, and to Arrabal, is confirmed by Bernard Gille in his book *Arrabal* (Paris: Éditions Seghers, 1970), p. 85. In alchemical terms, the interaction in the egg which transforms the *Materia Prima* into gold involves sulphur (solar, hot ,and male) and mercury (lunar, cold and female). See Orenstein's book (*op. cit.*), and Stanislas Klossowski de Rola's *Alchemy: The Secret Art* (New York: Bounty Books, 1973), p. 11.

27. Arrabal's educational background included the study of the Spanish theater of the Golden Age. He was particularly intrigued by Calderón's *La vida es sueño (Life is a Dream)* and in all probability was familiar with the latter dramatist's "auto sacramental," *El gran teatro del mundo (The Great Theater of the World).*

28. Orenstein, p. 249.

29. The Theater of Fernando Arrabal, Ph.D. diss., Ohio State 1970, p. 43.

30. *Ibid.*, p. 176.

31. The short story "Las ruinas circulares" ("The Circular Ruins") would be a particularly good example of this. It is found in English translation in the collection of Borges' writing titled *Labyrinths* (New York: New Directions Publishing Co., 1964).

32. "The Psychological Base of Arrabal's *L'Architecte et l'Empereur d'Assyrie*," *The French Review,* Special Issue, 45, 4 (1972), p. 125.

33. See Carl Jung's *Collected Works*, Vol. V (New York: Bollingen Foundation, 1956), pp. 208–16.

34. Lyons, p. 130.

35. *Loc. cit.*

36. See Dorothy Knowles' article "Ritual Theater: Fernando Arrabal and the Latin Americans," *Modern Language Review,* 70, No. 3 (July, 1975), 526–38, for a description of various productions of Arrabal's plays directed by the Argentines, Lavelli, Savary and García. A consideration of the lighting effects for the García production of *The Architect and the Emperor of Assyria* is found in Brian Arnott's article *"The Architect and the Emperor of Assyria:* A Scenography of Light," *The Drama Review* (Visual Performance Issue), 17, No. 2 (1973), 73–79.

37. Consult his article "Arrabal et le jeu dramatique des échecs," *Littérature,* 9 (1973), 101–17.

38. There is a danger inherent in stressing the significance of this scene.

Notes and References

Notes and References   155

In the Spanish version of the play, rather than dressing as The Bishop of Chess to enact his death, the Emperor appears as an ice cream pop. Thus, the chess motif wasn't present in the original conception of the play.

39. Chromaticism is a musical device in which the composer does not allow a key signature to establish itself. The constant use of additional sharps or flats denies the listener a feeling of repose; the music is never permitted to return to its harmonic "home base." This device captures an unresolved yearning of the characters concluded only in the final chords of the "Liebestod" or "Love Death" where their passion is resolved in death. The Emperor's inner turmoil, highlighted by the constant return of the mother motif, causes a similar feeling of "musical" tension throughout the play.

40. Quoted in Francis Ferguson's book, *The Idea of a Theater* (New York: Anchor Books, 1953), p. 84.

41. Schifres, p. 103.

42. *Ibid.*, p. 152.

43. *The Architect and the Emperor of Assyria* (New York: Grove Press, 1969), p. 21.

44. In *The Architect,* the element of ritual is taken directly from religion. It reaches its climax in the scene where the Emperor is devoured by the Architect. Arrabal is especially fond of blasphemous parodies; here the hint of the Transubstantiation produces a dramatic tension enhanced by the grotesque nature of its visual representation. The dramatic qualities of the Mass impressed themselves on Arrabal's mind from childhood, and he frequently seeks to transpose those qualities into his own plays, often mocking the traditional ritual.

45. Review of a performance of *The Architect and the Emperor of Assyria, The New York Times,* May 30, 1976.

46. Orenstein, p. 245.

47. *The Exploding Stage* (New York: Weybright and Talley, 1971), p. 103.

48. *Théâtre,* Vol. V (Paris: Christian Bourgois, 1969), p. 47.

49. Consult Françoise Espinasse's interview with Arrabal in *Théâtre III* (Paris: Christian Bourgois, 1969), p. 11, for a statement by Arrabal confirming this view of his imprisonment.

50. Messerman, p. 227.

51. For an analysis of the symbol of the bird with its padlocked beak consult Orenstein, p. 260.

52. Orenstein, p. 22.

53. Some of these refer to previous works. *The Labyrinth* is evoked by the servants' claim the Lys is a tyrant who beats them and the disappearance of the marks on their backs when Fridigan confronts her with that accusation. In another instance, Arrabal's stage directions refer back to a page in the text that is to be repeated *in toto* (on page 80 of Vol. VIII of *Théâtre*, Paris: christian Bourgois, 1970, Arrabal specifies that page 33 is

to be repeated). Subsequent references to this play will be taken from the edition cited.

54. Orenstein, p. 263.

55. On page 73 of *Ars Amandi* Arrabal describes one of those paintings; it is a giant pipe with the inscription "This is not a Pipe" and is to be reproduced on stage as part of the set.

56. Several works of Goya are reproduced in the form of stage images. In one instance (p. 71), Arrabal describes Lys' position by referring to Goya's painting *The Naked Maja*. And on page 66, Lys is seen in the air gesticulating grotesquely in a manner suggestive of Goya's painting of a mannequin being tossed into the air from a blanket.

57. See Orenstein, p. 268. The motif of the sky falling is also reminiscent of Artaud's short play *The Jet of Blood*.

58. Orenstein, p. 267.

59. *Love in the Western World* (New York: Pantheon Books, Inc., 1956), p. 21.

60. Review of Arrabal's *Théâtre VI* (Paris: Christian Bourgois, 1969), in *French Review,* Vol. 43, No. 4 (March, 1970), p. 727.

61. The extreme nature of the characters' "love-insults" illustrates the playwright's strong sense of black humor. A few examples will suffice; as Alima's passion grows in intensity, she tells Asan: "What we have between our toes, you undoubtedly have between your fingers" (p. 135). She later adds: "You have the brain of a mosquito that had been stricken with meningitis . . . you reason like a casserle filled with turnips" (p. 140).

62. Alima— You are filled with freshness, the sea sleeps
around your body.

Asan — You are the dream of ships.

Alima — We shall explode and God will preside over our
union.   (p. 144)

63. Luce was suffering from a grave illness during the time the play was written.

64. From inside the tortoise, Malik's voice is heard saying: "I have the impression of being here for nine months and of having been born several seconds ago into a new life . . . I have seen my life since the first day as if it were another's. I have witnessed my birth, I have seen my father who was playing the harp and the small car drawn by a panther and a goat" (*Théâtre VI*, p. 181). In Malik's dream during the early stages of his imprisonment he saw himself would Liska with a phallic knife, resulting in the birth from her head of a child (p. 154).

65. See Chapter 1, footnote 20, for the source of Arrabal's statement equating his imprisonment with "rebirth" and rediscovery of the true significance of his father.

66. Sigmund Freud, *A General Introduction to Psychoanalysis* (New York: Washington Square Press, 1961), p. 165.

67. (New York: Grove Press, 1958).

Chapter Four

1. *Sociology of Literature and Drama* (New York: Penguin Books, 1973), p. 76.

2. Arrabal himself is partial to Marxist literary criticism, especially as practiced by the French critic, Lucien Goldmann. Two books devoted to Arrabal's theater that should soon be in print utilize that critical perspective. They are Ángel Berenguer's *L'Exil et la Cérémonie dans le Premier Théâtre d'Arrabal,* a revision of his dissertation prepared under Goldmann, and José Ortega's *Aproximación al teatro de Arrabal.*

3. An "opuscule" is a pamphlet, and "groupuscule" was the name of one of the small activist groups in Paris during the Spring of 1968.

4. The English translation of this play is by Bettina Knapp; it was published in *The Drama Review,* No. 4 (Summer, 1969). The quotation included in the text of this study is found on page 128 of that issue.

5. Consult Ruby Cohn's review of these plays in *The French Review,* 45 (1975), 182–84, for a rather negative critique of *The Red and Black Dawn.*

6. Mel Gussow, "Arrabal — A Storm over the Wounded," *New York Times,* May 10, 1972, p. 40.

7. Clive Barnes, "Theater: Arrabal's 'Handcuffs' Shouts with Anger and Anguish," *New York Times,* April 22, 1972, p. 39.

8. Consult Charles Marowitz's article "Arrabal's Theater of Panic," *New York Times Magazine,* December 3, 1972, for an account of some of these excesses. At one point, the production was suspended until Arrabal promised that the actors would desist from biting the spectators.

9. This trio of male characters, which includes a mute (Pronos), suggests the Marx brothers. Their counterparts can be found in a number of Arrabal's early plays. But here the parallel acquires a bitterly ironic quality in light of the situation of the men.

10. *And They Put Handcuffs on the Flowers* (New York: Grove Press Inc., 1973), p. 30. A portion of the prayer is as follows: "Oh, God, I can no longer see, but my pleasure is all the greater. Oh, what joy to eat my own balls. And not to be able to see. All my enjoyment is concentrated in my mouth, my tongue — the mouth you gave me, Lord. The Lord giveth balls and the Lord taketh them away. Blessed be the name of the Lord."

11. This is quite evident in the critical reception accorded the New York production of the play (also directed by the author). Clive Barnes gave it a rave review. But Eric Bentley, in *The New York Times* of the following Sunday (April 23, 1972), attacked the entire venture vitriolically in an article entitled, "Time for the Audience to Shout Back."

12. In the original French version of the work, a celestial chorus is heard when the urine changes into blood; the "miracle" allows the drama to end on a decidedly optimistic note. But the English translation and the

New York production, both directed by Arrabal himself, suppress the final apotheosis, changing an optimistic conclusion into an ambiguous one.

13. The stage directions specify that a spectator be recruited to witness the performance in an iron collar while another is to view it from inside a cage. Then, after the play's conclusion, the two spectators are to share their feelings with the cast and the audience.

14. *Le Ciel et la Merde* (Paris: Christian Bourgois, 1972), p. 25. All subsequent references will be taken from this, the sole extant version of the work.

15. The musical quality of this scene is strongly reminiscent of the final scene in Richard Strauss' opera, *Salome*. The decadence and perversity of the scene in which Salome is presented with the severed head of John the Baptist and begins to kiss its lips were probably not a direct inspiration for Arrabal's play, but the similarity between the two is striking.

16. The name Cleaver is undoubtedly borrowed from Eldridge Cleaver, black militant leader, enlightened prisoner and political exile who authored the moving autobiography, *Soul on Ice*.

17. One of the examples Arrabal especially likes to proffer in affirming the link between Spanish Catholicism and sado-masochism is Saint Theresa's cry to God to penetrate her with a fiery sword. That is the basis of his identification of her with the Marquis de Sade.

18. Perhaps the most vivid example is Ribla's vision in which she lays a big egg in a nest from which the Messiah hatches. She then gives it cod-liver oil and spinach and it becomes a "Popeye God" (p. 69).

19. Arrabal himself repudiates the work in an introductory note to the published text: "I ask myself why I have written this abomination. If anyone can give me an explanation.... Write me!"

20. The victims mentioned include Kennedy, Lorca, Gandhi, Che Guevara, Mussolini, Lumumba, Trotsky, Rosa Luxembourg, Brasillach Jaures, and Martin Luther King.

21. Published together with *Le Ciel et la Merde*, p. 179.

22. Review of *Théâtre IX* in *French Review*, No. 2 (December, 1973), p. 483.

23. Consult pages 119–22.

24. *The Naked Image* (New York: The MacMillan Company, 1967), p. 52.

25. *The Theater of Revolt* (Boston: Little, Brown & Company, 1962), p. 259.

26. Arrabal explains this in his preface to the text (Paris: Christian Bourgois, 1972). All references to *The Thousand Year War* will be taken from this edition.

27. "Bella ciao" is the subtitle of the play. Arrabal has underscored the universality of the revolt by switching to another language (Italian) for this climactic song.

28. Friedrich Luft, "An Arrabal Premiere in Berlin," *Encounter,* XL, No. 1 (January, 1973), p. 94.

29. Consult Bettina Knapp's Inverview with Jérôme Savary, "Sounding the Drum," *Drama Review,* 15, No. 1 (Fall, 1970), 92–96, for a discussion of his "Magic Circus" and a consideration of his production of Arrabal's play, *The Labyrinth.*

30. *La marcha real* in *Literatura española del último exilio,* Antonio Ferres and José Ortega, eds. (New York: Gordian Press, 1975), p. 19. The play has been published subsequently in French as a part of Arrabal's complete theater (Paris: Christian Bourgois, 1976).

31. The idea that the route to bliss and virtue must pass through mud and excrement has been encountered in a number of previous plays, most notably *Ars Amandi* and *Erotic Bestiality.*

32. The play was published by Christian Bourgois in 1974 in a bilingual French-Spanish edition. Despite the poor job of editing the Spanish text, I have used the version because of my own Hispanic orientation and because Arrabal still initially composes his plays in Spanish. This particular reference is taken from page 88. All subsequent quotations from the drama will be taken from the Spanish text.

33. The Duke says to Wichita: "I'm not speaking of your Madrid, of this Madrid where we are now, I'm speaking of a rancid, rotten Madrid planted in the center of Spain like a boil on the flesh of a leper" (p. 76).

34. The tuberculosis Arrabal had developed in Spain represented for him the physiological manifestation of emotions produced by life in that country. Paradoxically, the disease completely incapacitated him only when he left Spain for France in 1955.

35. Pp. 90–91.

36. Scott Sullivan, "The Wire's Edge," *Newsweek,* November 11, 1975.

37. All of the names of the male characters in the play come from Lewis Carroll. Tenniel is the name of the famous illustrator of *Alice in Wonderland* and *Through the Looking Glass* (consult *The Annotated Alice,* introduction and notes by Martin Gardner [New York: Bramhall House, 1960] for the complete illustrations). The mysterious Snarck is found in Carroll's poem "The Hunting of the Snarck" in *Poems of Lewis Carroll* (New York: Thomas Y. Crowell Co., 1973).

38. These words, taken from the last chapter of Kafka's *Amerika,* were also used to introduce Arrabal's play, *The Labyrinth.*

39. This situation echoes that of the British film, *The Loneliness of the Long Distance Runner,* with Tom Courtenay, in which the protagonist declines to cross the finish line in a race as a gesture of his socio-political feelings.

40. Tenniel's illustration of the Knight of Chess which introduces *Through the Looking Glass* is clearly modeled on Cervantes' famous character.

41. *Les jeunes barbares d'aujourd'hui* (Paris: Christian Bourgois, 1975), p. 10. All subsequent references to this drama will be taken from this, the only extant edition of the work.

42. José Bellido, a Spanish underground dramatist, has written a short drama based entirely on just such a metaphor. Although I am not certain if Arrabal was acquainted with Bellido's *Football,* it does appear in English translation together with Arrabal's *Solemn Communion* (translated *First Communion* in the volume) in George Wellwarth and Michael Benedikt's collection of plays, *Modern Spanish Drama* (New York: E. P. Dutton and Co., 1969).

43. *Op. cit.,* p. 40.

44. The historical Gilles de Rais entered the service of Charles VII in 1429 and was made responsible by the king's chief minister, Georges de la Trémouille, for the safety of Joan of Arc (hence the association of the two in the play). Gilles remained with her from the relief of Orléans in May, 1429, to the time of her capture by the Burgundians at Compiègne in May, 1430.

45. *La Gloire en Images* in *La Tour de Babel, Théâtre XI* (Paris: Christian Bourgois, 1976), p. 104. All subsequent references to this play will be taken from this same source.

46. The Devil appears as a goat in Goya's famous painting, *Aquelarre* (*Witches' Sabbath*).

47. Arrabal told me of his fondness for this opera in discussion held on February 15, 1977. The previous year, a controversial production of the work in Paris under the direction of Jorge Lavelli outraged many tradition-minded operagoers by omitting the *Walpurgisnacht* ballet. For that reason, it is quite possible that Arrabal had the scene in mind when he created his own ballet. In any case, the similarities in tone between the two scenes are striking.

48. Puppets are closely associated with the grotesque mode in art and literature. Important studies analyzing this feature of the grotesque include Wolfgang Kayser's *The Grotesque in Art and Literature* (Bloomington: Indiana University Press, 1963), Frances K. Barasch's *The Grotesque: A Study in Meanings* (The Hague: Mouton, 1971) and Philip Thomson's *The Grotesque* (London: Methuen and Co., 1972). For a consideration of the grotesque mode in Arrabal's work, consult my study "The Psychological Origins and the Sociological Dimension of the Grotesque in the Works of Fernando Arrabal," *Estreno,* 2, No. 1 (1975), 21–26, or Roger Benoit's "The Grotesque in the Theater of Fernando Arrabal" (Unpublished dissertation, University of Kansas, 1975).

49. Teran is the family name of Arrabal's mother.

50. The ass is a symbol of the realm of the marvelous and of the salvation through art which resides there. In some ways, it is similar to the tortoise in *A Tortoise Named Dostoievsky.*

51. "La Pasionaria" was the name earned by Dolores Ibarurri for her

eloquence as a speaker during the Civil War. The Spanish Communist leader returned to her native land on May 13, 1977, after living thirty-eight years in exile in the Soviet Union. She was noted for her impassioned battlecry "No pasarán" ("They shall not pass") repeated here by Latidia in the play.

52. This situation suggests the position of the Spanish government during Arrabal's imprisonment in 1967.

53. This concept is succinctly summarized by the title *Heaven and Shit,* and is encountered in a number of previous dramas.

54. This same episode with a black pearl is contained in the panic prose poem, *La Pièrre de la Folie* (Paris: Rene Julliard, 1963). In this work the pearl is extracted from the neck of the author-narrator; thus indirectly the existence of the earlier work intensifies the association between Arrabal and Latidia.

55. *La Tour de Babel,* p. 63.

56. *The Architect and the Emperor of Assyria* has been performed in Barcelona in April, 1977, and *The Car Cemetery* and *The Tower of Babel* were presented in Madrid during that same year.

Chapter Five

1. Richard Howard, translator of *Baal Babylon* (New York: Grove Press, 1961); this statement appears on the rear cover of the book.

2. *Loc. cit.*

3. *Loc. cit.*

4. *The Craft of Fiction* (London: Jonathan Cape, 1921), p. 127.

5. *Baal Babylon,* p. 41. All subsequent quotations from this novel will be taken from the above-cited translation by R. Howard.

6. For an analysis of the role of the mother figure in Arrabal's work, consult Phyllis Boring's article, "Arrabal's Mother Image," *Kentucky Romance Quarterly,* 15 (1968), 285–92.

7. *L'Enterrement de la sardine* (Paris: Christian Bourgeois, 1970), p. 134. Subsequent references to this novel will be taken from this edition of the work.

8. There are several references to the Anglican pastor, Reverend Dodgson. The first appears on page 20 of the text. Lewis Carroll is the pen name of the Reverend Charles Dodgson. His fondness for little girls is reflected by the fictional character's photographing of nude young girls.

9. Examples include a man with a rat's head (Chapter 9) and a bird with two human heads (Chapter 11). The grotesque dominates the aesthetic of the entire novel. The carnival in the street includes a myriad of crippled and deformed people (e.g., a one-armed old lady on stilts). Their prominent place in the work and the visual quality of the descriptions suggest the medium of cinema and two directors specifically: Alexandro Jodorowsky (*El topo*) and Federico Fellini. Both utilize dwarfs, cripples,

and people with other anomalies in their films. The literary utilization of hybrids composed of human, animal and vegetable elements has been identified as an essential feature of the grotesque from its very origins as an artistic mode. Among the studies considering such hybrids are: Wolfgang Kayser, *The Grotesque in Art and Literature* (Bloomington: Indiana University Press, 1963) and Frances K. Barasch, in the introduction to Thomas Wright's *A History of Caricature and Grotesque in Literature and Art* (New York: Frederick Ungar Publishing Co., 1968).

10. The levels of dream which constitute life and the circular design of our existence are important aspects of modern art. They figure prominently in the short stories of Jorge Luis Borges and the paintings and graphics of Maurits Cornelius Escher.

11. Françoise Raymond-Mundschau, *Arrabal* (Paris: Editions Universitaires, 1972), p. 99.

12. This sort of birth is associated with myth; in Greek mythology Minerva sprang full-grown from the head of her father, Zeus. Arrabal also utilizes the Arabian myth of the Phoenix, a bird that sets itself afire and then from out of its ashes returns to life. (The Phoenix has become associated with alchemy.) In *Rites and Celebration of Confusion,* Arrabal integrates into the work's content several of the dream-like paintings he commissioned. (Photos of several are included in the novel.) One such painting, "The Birth of Arrabal," shows the enormous face of the playwright, mouth open, releasing a smaller, naked Arrabal with mouth open producing yet another identical but smaller copy of the author, *ad infinitum.* The painting unites a humorous reference to the advertising symbol of a French cheese, "La vache qui rit," with the essence of the above-mentioned myths.

13. The painting is included in the edition of the text cited. It shows the author standing and pointing with his finger to his mouth. His entire chest and abdomen have been opened to reveal his organs. The foreground and background of the painting are divided by two columns. Alongside of each, in small boxes, are the fourteen images representing various parts of the author's body. These include a ship trapped in a cage (his head); a trunk and the sun with human features (his eyes); a centaur and an animal, half cat, half fish (his feet); a knight of chess in an open field (his legs); two enormous fingers pressed together and pierced by an arrow (his arms) and so forth.

14. Northrop Frye claims that all literary genres are derived from the single myth of quest — consult his *Anatomy of Criticism* (Princeton: Princeton University Press, 1957), pp. 192–96. Wayne Booth alludes to the modern quest-novel which has been utilized in various ways by many of our most important contemporary novelists, including Joyce, Proust, Mann and Kafka; consult Booth's *The Rhetoric of Fiction* (Chicago: The University of Chicago Press, 1961). Much of Arrabal's work, his plays as well as his novels, can be related to some extent to this central myth; it is

particularly important in *Rites and Celebrations of Confusion.*

15. In the episode, the narrator falls asleep during an airplane trip and dreams he is overcome by an irrational and uncontrollable impulse and stabs a man he had known during his childhood. Upon awakening, he is reassured to find himself seated in the plane; but when it lands all passengers are instructed to exit by a side door because someone has been stabbed. The victim's name proves to be that of the narrator's childhood friend.

16. In this labyrinth, her body is a mirror deforming Arrabal's image; the mirror in the dining room shows a man with a hunting gun who mimicks all of Arrabal's movements. When Arrabal expresses frustration at what he sees, the girl breaks the dining room mirror and abruptly ceases to reflect images herself. The idea of woman as mirror has a touch of Sartrean existential anguish; man cannot see himself as he believes himself to be, but rather is confronted with a distortion of his image reflected in the eyes of the female — hence the pain he feels at not conforming to his own expectations and view of himself.

17. Another of Arrabal's plays is reproduced in the novel; the thirty-fifth labyrinth corresponds to the short Panic drama, *Illustrious Youth.*

18. Gloria Orenstein, *The Theater of the Marvelous* (New York: New York University Press, 1975), p. 251.

19. *Fêtes et Rites de la Confusion* (Paris: Eric Losfeld, 1967), pp. 184–85.

20. *The Theory of the Novel* (Cambridge: Massachusetts Institute of Technology Press, 1971), p. 89.

Chapter Six

1. The film's title was the Nationalist's battle cry during the Civil War. It was coined by General Millán Astray and shouted by him during his historical confrontation with Miguel de Unamuno in Salamanca in 1936.

2. For a consideration of the differences between the novel and the film which transcend what can be explained by the characteristics of the two media, consult either my study, "Fernando Arrabal and *Viva la muerte,*" *West Coast Review,* XI, No. 2 (October, 1976), 3–6, or David Whitton's "*Viva la muerte:* a Film by Arrabal," *Durham University Journal,* XXXIV, No. 2 (March, 1973), 201–04.

3. This technique consisted of shooting with 35 mm. black and white film and then transferring each sequence onto a two inch wide strip of magnetic tape. Garish shades of red, green, and blue are then introduced as the film is viewed through a television monitor.

4. Topor is a friend of Arrabal's and one of the founders of the Panic movement.

5. The role of the adult Fando was played by Víctor García, the avant-garde director who has worked on numerous productions of Arrabal's plays. "Fando," a variation of Arrabal's first name, Fernando, has been

utilized by him for a number of the male protagonists with whom he identifies.

6. In reality, Arrabal's hospitalization for tuberculosis occurred in 1955 when he was twenty-three years of age. This transposition of the experience to his childhood is in keeping with his treatment of time and memory throughout the film.

7. Arrabal's films are available for rental from New Line Cinema in New York City. *I Would Go Like a Crazy Horse* has not been released in the United States. I understand that the copy which New Line was to get was accidentally destroyed. To date, I have been unable to see the film. My presentation of the work here, of necessity quite brief, is based on Ángel Berenguer's interesting study, "La segunda película de Arrabal," *Triunfo,* No. 583 (December 15, 1973), 72–73.

8. The pranks include telling children that the hosts in church are poisoned, painting a woman performing fellatio on the crucified Christ, and bursting in on a meeting of the Spanish Royal Academy to mock their procedures.

9. In the film, the doves come to symbolize peace and brotherhood among men.

10. Arrabal told this to me during a discussion held on May 31, 1976.

11. Certain factual horrors of the Civil War find their way into a number of Arrabal's works. This episode also appears in *And They Put Handcuffs on the Flowers* and is mentioned in the *Letter to General Franco.*

12. All of Arrabal's works published in French are listed by category in the Christian Bourgois editions.

13. Other allusions include the author-protagonist's sleeping with and strangling a female doll (*The Grand Ceremonial*), his transporting his girl friend in a baby carriage and showing off her physical charms to other men (*Fando and Lis*), and his being trapped in a latrine amidst a maze of sheets (*The Labyrinth*).

14. The idea of the union of opposites appears in one episode in which, as Arrabal writes the word RIEN (NOTHING) on a paper, he sees the phosphorescent letters TOUT (EVERYTHING) on his thumb (p. 16). In another episode, the narrator and a girl enter an egg (the alchemical oven) and metamorphose into a single body with two heads (p. 110).

15. Examples include *The Birth of Arrabal* (inspired by the commercials for the French cheese, "La vache qui rit"), a painting based on an advertisement for undergarments, and the 1963 version of *Arrabal combatting his Megalomania* (copied from a page in the dictionary and Goya's *The Burial of the Sardine).*

16. *La carta al general Franco* (Paris: Union Générale d'Éditions, 1972), p. 103.

17. In my discussion with Arrabal on May 31, 1976, he spoke of his great love for New York, indicating that if he were not to take his wife's

preferences and obligations into consideration he might well choose to live there.

Chapter Seven

1. In *Entretiens avec Arrabal,* p. 22, the author recounts how he sought to make each new work entirely different; however, his wife's comment, after examining each successive effort was always: "Despite the novelty of the play, I still decidedly detect once again your presence in the piece."

2. It should be noted that Arrabal is one of the very few Spanish authors writing about Spanish themes to achieve worldwide recognition. That achievement raises several interesting questions. First: should Arrabal be considered Spanish or French? Second: would he have achieved the renown he now enjoys had he not left his native country? My own Hispanic allegiance provides my answer, "Spanish," to the first question. As for the second, I feel, as I am sure Arrabal agrees, that his success in projecting Spanish concerns and methodologies (use of blasphemy and black humor) in a manner captivating to the interest of an international audience was due largely to Arrabal's unique blend of a Spanish background with the freedom of intellectual and artistic stimulation encountered in Paris. It is precisely this combination which has enabled Arrabal to develop into the sort of dramatist he has become.

Selected Bibliography

PRIMARY SOURCES

I In French

1. Editions Julliard:

Théâtre I (*Oraison, Les Deux Bourreaux, Fando et Lis, Le Cimetière des Voitures* — 1958)

Théâtre II (*Guernica, Le Labyrinthe, Le Tricycle, Pique-nique en campagne, La Bicyclette du condamné* — 1961)

Théâtre III (*Le Couronnement, Le Grand Ceremonial, Cérémonie pour un Noir assassiné* — 1965)

Baal Babylone (1959)

L'Enterrement de la sardine (1961)

La Pierre de la Folie (1963)

2. Christian Bourgois:

Théâtre I (Reedition of Julliard, 1968)

Théâtre II (Reedition of Julliard, 1968)

Théâtre III (*Le Grand Cérémonial, Cérémonie pour un Noir assassiné* — 1969)

Théâtre IV (*Le Couronnement, Concert dans un oeuf* — 1969)

Theâtre V (*Théâtre panique, L'Architecte et l'Empereur D'Assyrie*, 1967)

Théâtre VI (*Le Jardin des délices, Bestialité érotique, Une tortue nommée Dostoievski* — 1969)

Théâtre VII (*Et ils Passèrent des menottes aux fleurs, L'Aurore rouge et noire* — 1969)

Théâtre VIII (Deux opéras paniques: *Ars Amandi, Dieu tenté par les mathématiques* — 1970)

Théâtre IX (*Le Ciel et la Merde, La grande revue du XXe Siècle* — 1972)

Théâtre X (*La Guerre de mille ans*, 1972, *Sur le Fil* ou *Ballade du train fant7ome*, 1974, *Jeunes barbares d'aujourd'hui*, 1975)

Théâtre XI (*La Tour de Babel, La Marche Royale, Une Orange sur le Mont de Vénus, La Gloire en Images* — 1976).

L'Enterrement de la sardine (1970).

La pierre de la folie (1970).

167

3. Other Publishers:

Lettre au Général Franco. Paris: Union Générale d'Editions, 1972.
Sur Fischer. Paris: Editions du Rocher, 1974.
Le New York d'Arrabal. Paris: Andre Balland, 1973.
Fêtes et Rites de la Confusion. Paris: Eric Losfeld, 1967.
La Pierre de la Folie and *Cent Sonnets* (Melzer Verlag).

II   In Spanish

El cementerio de automóviles, Ciugrena, Los dos verdugos. Madrid: Taurus, 1965.
El triciclo. Madrid: Escelicer, 1965, and in *Yorick* No. 8, Barcelona, 1965.
Fando y Lis in *Yorick,* No. 15, Barcelona, 1966, and Madrid: Escelicer, 1967.
Arrabal celebrando la ceremonia de la confusión. Madrid: Alfaguara, 1966.
Oración in *Primer acto,* No. 39, January, 1963, 46–48.
Ceremonia para un negro asesinado in *Primer acto,* No. 74, April, 1966, 33–48.
El laberinto in *Revista Mundo Nuevo,* No. 15, September, 1967.
La primera comunión in *Revista los Esteros,* 1967.
Oración, Los dos verdugos and *El cementerio de automóviles* in Teatro I Paris: Christian Bourgois, 1971.
Carta al general Franco. Paris: Union Générale d'Editions, 192.
Viva la muerte (Baal Babylone). Madrid: Tiempo Contemporáneo, 1974.
Ceremonia para una cabra sobre una nube. Málaga: Curso Superior de Filología de Málaga, 1974.
En la cuerda o La balada del tren fantasma. Paris: Christian Bourgois, 1974.
La marcha real in *Literatura española del último exilio,* eds. Antonio Ferres and José Ortega. New York: Gordian Press, 1975, pp. 16–24.
El arquitecto y el emperador de Assyria in *Estreno,* 2, 1, 1975, T1–T28 (an error in the manuscript was corrected in *Estreno,* 3, 1, 1977, pp. 6–7).
Pic-Nic. El triciclo. El Laberinto Edition and introduction by Ángel Berenguer. Madrid: Ediciones Cátedra, 1977.
La Balada del tren fantasma in *Pipirijaina,* No. 4.

III   In English

1. New York: Grove Press:

*Baal Babylon.*Trans. Richard Howard, 1961.
*Guérnica and Other Plays (The Labyrinth, the Tricycle, Picnic on the Battlefield),*Trans. Barbara Wright, 1969.
The Architect and the Emperor of Assyria, Trans. Everard d'Harnoncourt and Adele Shank, 1969.

And They Put Handcuffs on the Flowers. Trans. Charles Marowitz, 1973.
Garden of Delights. Trans. Helen and Tom Bishop, 1974.

2. London: Calder and Boyars:

Plays (Orison, The Two Executioners, Fando and Lis, The Car Cemetery — 1962).
The Burial of the Sardine — 1965).
Plays, Volume II (Guérnica, The Labyrinth, The Tricycle, Picnic on the Battlefield, The Condemned Man's Bicycle — 1967).
Plays, Volume III (The Architect and the Emperor of Assyria, The Grand Ceremonial, The Solemn Communion — 1970).

3. Others:

Solemn Communion, Strip Tease of Jealousy, Impossible Loves. The Drama Review, 13, 1968.
The Groupuscule of My Heart in *The Drama Review.* Trans. Bettina Knapp, No. 4 (Summer, 1969), 123–28.
First Communion in *Modern Spanish Theater.* eds. Michael Benedikt and George Wellwarth. New York: E. P. Dutton & Co., 1969, 309–17.
Picnic on the Battlefield in *Evergreen Review.* 4, Trans. James Hewitt, No. 15, November–December, 1960, 76–90.

IV   Interviews

"Auto-interview." *The Drama Review,* 13 (1968), 73–76.
Espinasse Françoise in Théâtre III. Paris: Christian Bourgois, 1969, 7–22.
Knapp Bettina. "Interview with Arrabal." *First Stage,* 6, No. 4 (Winter 1967-1968), 198–201.
Monleón. José "Arrabal y Latinoamérica." *Primer Acto,* No. 174 (November, 1974), 58–64.
Morrissett. Ann "Dialogue with Arrabal." *Evergreen Review,* IV, No. 15 (November-December 1960), 70–75.
Munk. Erika "The Director Has No Clothes." *The Village Voice* (June 14, 1976) p. 125.
Schifres. Alain *Entretiens avec Arrabal.* Paris: Editions Pierre Belfond, 1969.

V   Essays of Arrabal

"La alienación franquista." *Estreno,* 2, No. 1 (1975), 9–10.
"L'entropie et ses ravages" in *Théâtre XI,* Paris: Christian Bourgois, 1976, pp. 11–14.
"El hombre pánico" with the plays *El cementerio, Ciugrena, Los dos verdugos.* Madrid: Taurus 1965, pp. 31–44.

"L'Homme panique" in *Le Panique.* Paris: Union générale d'éditions, 1973, pp. 37–53.

"Le nouveau 'nouveau théâtre' " in *Théâtre XI.* Paris: Christian Bourgois, 1976, pp. 7–10.

"Le théâtre comme cérémonie panique" in *Le panique, op. cit.,* pp. 97–100.

SECONDARY SOURCES

ANDERSON, IRMGARD. "From Tweedledum and Tweedledee to Zapo and Zepo." *Romance Notes,* XV, No. 2 (Winter, 1973), pp. 217–20. An analysis of *Picnic on the Battlefield* that seeks to demonstrate Arrabal's debt to the chapter "Tweedledum and Tweedledee" in Lewis Carroll's *Through the Looking Glass.*

BERENGUER, ANGEL. "La segunda película de Arrabal." *Triunfo,* No. 583 (December 15, 1973), pp. 72–73. A sociological interpretation of the film *I Would Go Like a Crazy Horse.*

BORING, PHYLLIS. "Arrabal's Mother Image." *Kentucky Romance Quarterly,* 15 (1968), pp. 285–92. An analysis of the mother figure and her symbolization of church and state in Arrabal's works.

COHN, RUBY. *Currents in Contemporary Drama.* Bloomington: Indiana University Press, 1969. Arrabal's drama in the context of contemporary theater.

DE LONG-TONELLI, BEVERLY. "Bicycles and Balloons in Arrabal's Dramatic Structure." *Modern Drama,* 14 (1971), pp. 205–09. An excellent study of the structure and meaning of *The Condemned Man's Bicycle* in terms of the two central symbols of the bicycle and the balloon.

DÍAZ, JANET. "Theater and Theories of Fernando Arrabal." *Kentucky Romance Quarterly,* 16 (1969), pp. 143–54. A fine general article on Arrabal, his plays, novels and paintings, and the writers and artists who influenced him.

ESSLIN, MARTIN. *The Theater of the Absurd.* Revised edition. New York: Anchor Books, 1969, pp. 217–22. A consideration of Arrabal's early plays in light of Esslin's concept of the theater of the absurd.

GILLE, BERNARD. *Arrabal.* Paris: Editions Seghers, 1970. A good general study of Arrabal's theater, complete with chronology, bibliography, photos and analyses of individual plays.

GUICHARNAUD, JACQUES. "Forbidden Games: Arrabal." *Yale French Studies,* 29 (1962), pp. 116–20. An analysis of the sources and themes of Arrabal's early plays with an emphasis on the significance of the childlike characters of those works.

KILLINGER, JOHN. "Arrabal and Surrealism." *Modern Drama,* 14 (1971), pp. 210–23. An analysis of Arrabal's work in light of the principal characteristics of Surrealism.

KNOWLES, DOROTHY. "Ritual Theater: Fernando Arrabal and the Latin-Americans. " *Modern Language Review*, 70, No. 3 (July , 1975), pp. 526–38. An interesting description of some of the productions of Arrabal's plays directed by the Argentines: Lavelli, García, and Savary.

KRONIK, JOHN. "Arrabal and the Myth of Guernica." *Estreno*, 2, No. 1 (1975), pp. 15–20. An excellent study of the play *Guérnica* and its debt to Picasso's painting and the concept of spatial form in modern nonnaturalistic art.

LYONS, CHARLES. "The Psychological Base of Arrabal's *L'Architecte et l'Empereur d'Assyrie.*" *The French Review*, 45, No. 4 (1972), pp. 123–36. A well conceived Jungian analysis of *The Architect and the Emperor of Assyria.*

MENDELSON, DAVID. "Arrabal et le jeu dramatique des échecs." *Littérature*, IX (1973), pp. 101–17. A brilliant and complex analysis of *The Architect* on several levels, commencing with a presentation of the significance of chess to the work and considering its psychoanalytic, socio-historical and mythic aspects.

ORENSTEIN, GLORIA. *The Theater of the Marvelous.* New York: New York University Press, 1975. A fascinating study of the role of Surrealism in the theater of a number of contemporary dramatists. The book's consideration of the significance of alchemical symbols in contemporary drama is particularly enlightening. One chapter, "A Surrealist Theatrical Tractate: Fernando Arrabal," is devoted specifically to Arrabal, but the entire book is indispensable for the understanding of his Panic theater.

ORTEGA, JOSÉ. "El sentido de la obra de Fernando Arrabal." *Estreno*, 2, No. 1 (1975), pp. 11–13. A succinct but profound analysis of Arrabal's work from a psychological and sociological perspective.

PODOL, PETER. "The Psychological Origins and the Sociological Dimension of the Grotesque in the Works of Fernando Arrabal." *Estreno*, 2, No. 1 (1975), pp. 21–26.

_____. "Fernando Arrabal and *Viva la muerte.*" *West Coast Review*, 11, No. 2 (October, 1976), 3–6.

POLO DE BERNABÉ, JOSÉ. "Arrabal y los límites del teatro." *Kentucky Romance Quarterly*, 22, No. 4 (1975), pp. 459–71. An interesting overview of Arrabal's theater from a psychological and structural standpoint.

RAYMOND-MUNDSCHAU, FRANÇOISE. *Arrabal.* Paris: Editions Universitaires, 1972. A good general study of Arrabal's theater, with emphasis on the biographical and psychological components of his work.

SERREAU, GENEVIÈVE. "A New Comic Style: Arrabal." *Evergreen Review*, No. 15 (1960), pp. 61–69. Focuses on humor as an efficacious dramatic device in Arrabal's theater that serves him well in his quest for artistic and personal liberation.

THIHER, ALLEN. "Fernando Arrabal and the New Theater of Obsession." *Modern Drama*, 13 (1970), pp. 174–83. Focuses on ceremony and sadism in Arrabal's theater.

WHITTON, DAVID. "A Critical Edition of the Manuscript of the First Version of Arrabal's *Bicyclette du condamné.*" *Forum for Modern Language Studies*, 9 (1973), pp. 253–68.

————. "*Viva la muerte:* a film by Arrabal." *Durham University Journal*, 34, No. 2 (March, 1973), pp. 201–04.

ADDENDA I

Unpublished Dissertations in the United States

ANDERSON, IRMGARD. "Some Aspects of Biblical Influence upon the Absurdist Theater of Beckett, Ghelderode and Arrabal." (Univ. of Alabama, 1972).

BENOIT, ROGER. "The Grotesque in the Theater of Fernando Arrabal." (Univ. of Kansas, 1975).

DONAHUE, THOMAS. "Three Stages on Arrabal's Way." (Univ. of Pennsylvania, 1973).

GREENBAUM, FRANCES. "The Dramatic World of Fernando Arrabal: Chance, Conflict and Confusion." (Syracuse Univ., 1974).

GREENE, KATHLEEN. "Spanish Playwrights and the Theater of Cruelty: Valle-Inclán, García Lorca and Arrabal." (Univ. of Kentucky, 1976).

HONIGSBLUM, GERALD. "Le Théâtre d'Arrabal." (Univ. of Chicago, 1972).

JOYET, MICHEL. "La Dialectique du réel et de l'imaginaire dans l'oeuvre théâtrale d'Arrabal." (Univ. of California, Santa Cruz, 1972).

MESSERMAN, LOIS. "The Theater of Fernando Arrabal: A Garden of Earthly Delights." (Ohio State Univ., 1970).

OLSON, R. LOYDON. "Aspects of the World of Childhood in the Works of Arrabal." (Univ. of Rhode Island, 1967).

SAADI, ANTOINE. "Le Grand Cérémonial de Fernando Arrabal." (Case Western Reserve Univ., 1972).

SLATON, ALICE. "Le Théâtre de Fernando Arrabal." (Univ. of California at Los Angeles, 1975).

WOODS, LYNETTE. "Integration and Disintegration in the Dramatic Works of Fernando Arrabal." (Michigan State Univ., 1973).

ADDENDA II

Books in Preparation
(Not available in time to be consulted for this study)

BERENGUER, ANGEL. *L'Exil et la Cérémonie dans le Premier Théâtre d'Arrabal* (Paris: Union Générale d'Éditions).

BERENGUER, JOAN and ÁNGEL. *Arrabal* (Madrid: Fundamentos, Col. Espiral/Figuras).

CAPELO, REGIO. *Le Théâtre d'Arrabal* (Ed. Umana).

DAERWYLER, JEAN-JACQUES. *Arrabal* (La Cité—L'Age d'Homme).

ORTEGA, JOSÉ. *Aproximación al teatro de Arrabal.*

Index